Table of Contents

Copyright Notice	3
Disclaimer	3
Introduction	4
Getting Started	5
How to Begin with Little or No Money	10
Build your Business with Small Offices	11
Who are the Clients?	13
What About References?	14
License and Insurance Information	15
The Best Part-Time Employees	17
Basic Cleaning Supplies	21
Basic Equipment List	24
The Routine Cleaning	24
How to Correctly Figure the Monthly Bill	25
The Best Time to Bill the Office	30
A Sample Bill	31
An Introduction Letter	32
A Professional Service Agreement	35
Bid Follow-Up Letter	37
Reminder Letter	38
Square Foot Estimating Chart	39
Labor Time Estimate Guide	40
The Business is "Getting the Business"	42
The Best Proven Methods for Getting Customers	43
Key to Success in Your Own Cleaning Business	60
Creative Bidding Method Gets More Accounts	62
Price, Bid and Estimate for Maximum Profits	63
The Profit Range Factor Explained	65
The Ultimate Chart That Does the Selling for You	69
Exactly What to Say for Great Results	70
Word for word interviews with office managers	74
Writing Paychecks	84
Hire Employees or Subcontract?	86
Subcontractor Service Agreement	89
Organize and Expand your Prospect List	90
How to Keep Your Customers Loyal Regardless of the Competition	91
Cover sheet for your bid	95
Answers to the most Frequently Asked Questions?	97
Make Income from Cleaning Last a Lifetime	104
Overlooked Tax Deductions	110
Little Known Resources for your Cleaning Business	113

Conclusion... 115
4 Special Bonus Reports…………………………………………........... 120--146

Copyright Notice

Copyright © by Sam Rodman. All Rights Reserved. The "Instant Office Cleaning Kit" has been registered with the United States Library of Congress and is fully protected by the COPYRIGHT LAW OF THE UNITED STATES OF AMERICA contained in Title 17 of the United States Code.

No part of this information may be reproduced by any means, without the express written consent of the author and publisher, Sam Rodman. Purchasers of this kit may reproduce the forms, sales letters and service agreement in the kit with their own company name on them for personal use only in the operation of an actual office cleaning, janitorial type of service business. Unauthorized use of the sales letters and service agreement contained in this kit for resale purposes is strictly forbidden. **ISBN # 0974771104**

Note: The owner of this book is allowed to print ONE copy for his or her own use. Violations of this copyright will be enforced.

Disclaimer

This information is distributed with the understanding that the author and publisher are not engaged in rendering legal, accounting, or other professional advice. If legal advice or other expert assistance is required, the services of a competent professional should be sought.

Also note that this information in no way guarantees any specific amount of money to be made and the author, Sam Rodman cannot be held responsible for any actions that you the reader may take. The square foot prices, form letters, and information that I share with you in this Kit are the result of my many years of experience in the office cleaning business.

They represent my best knowledge of workable methods. There is no way to guarantee that the information will apply to your particular type of application. However, the information that follows does have a proven track record and is supplied to provide you with guidance. It is the user's sole responsibility to determine the applicability of the material to his or her use, and the author and publisher assume no responsibility for situations which may arise from the user's application of this material to his or her own cleaning service business.

However, the information that follows does have a proven track record and is supplied to provide you with guidance. It is the user's sole responsibility to determine the applicability of the material to his or her use, and the author and publisher assume no responsibility for situations which may arise from the user's application of this material to his or her own service business.

Introduction

This Kit describes practical, proven methods. Its purpose is to provide you with the necessary guidance and materials that will help you to obtain your own office cleaning accounts and the financial gain that comes from doing so.

The service of cleaning offices is here to stay. Many people have used the information contained in this Kit to get their own cleaning service started and increase their income. You can too!

The business of cleaning offices and maintaining their appearance is a service business like none other. I know of no other company where individual customers will pay you hundreds of dollars every month and in many cases, thousands of dollars every month for what amounts to just a few hours of your time and effort.

Can you actually earn yourself $70 to $75 dollars an hour or more for cleaning offices? The answer is yes, and I'm going to explain to you exactly how to get these customers for yourself. I know what I'm talking about.

Cleaning up is big business! The cleaning industry, in general, generates over 35 billion dollars every year in the United States, and you can get your share of this growing revenue. Of all the different types of cleaning services out there, office cleaning is the cream of the crop.

The United States Department of Commerce reported that over 11 billion dollars were spent last year, specifically, on commercial cleaning services and this cleaning service revenue which is increasing every year.

Office cleaning or so-called janitorial business is a profitable commercial cleaning service. It is a genuine recession-proof business, and you now have the information you need to profit from it.

Within a few miles from your home, there are many dollars of monthly office cleaning accounts waiting for you.

There are a few large national franchise companies in the janitorial business. The people who run these companies are just like you. They've just been in the business longer and have more employees and customers than you do at this time.

You can become one of the big companies too if you stay in this business long enough and you want to keep on growing.

Note: At the end of this kit (just before the 4 bonus reports) be sure to read about how you can make money from the office cleaning business, with or without starting your own cleaning service.

Getting Started

Many people in the office cleaning business started out as a little mom and pop service business, working out of a station wagon or the family car. Most of them do a much better job than the larger cleaning companies, and they get paid just as much money for doing it.

The fact is, you have a significant advantage over the larger cleaning companies. When you're just getting started, you can be on the job supervising as the office gets cleaned. A smaller cleaning company can do a much better job than a larger cleaning company.

Many office managers understand this fact and are receptive to hiring your cleaning service instead major companies for this very reason.

In the office cleaning business, the more accounts you take on, the more money you will make. Working part-time for a full-time income is typical in this business, and you can do it too.

There is a big misconception that a lot of people have about the office cleaning business. Janitorial work, in general, is thought of as a low-paying dead-end job.

You don't need to be a college graduate to empty trash cans, and most part-time employees of cleaning services are only paid a low hourly wage. In contrast, the owner of the private cleaning service, the one who put in the bid and got the account is getting paid a fixed amount of money every month.

This steady income usually translates into around $75 Dollars per cleaning, for an average of one hour of work. You are not some kind of low, hourly paid high school janitor. When you own the cleaning service company, you are considered to be a cleaning contractor.

There is no special license or exam to take. A cleaning contractor is a job title for the person who owns the cleaning service. If you have someone work with you and help you clean the office, (which you will most likely prefer), then you will make a little less, but it's still a lot of money for what usually amounts to one hour of work for one office.

There is a lot of work out there for anyone who goes after it, the right way.

All things considered, office cleaning is a good repeat service business to make money from, and you can do it. It's a profitable service business to get into, even if you don't want to do it full-time.

Chances are you will never do it full-time because the entire business is handled in the part-time evening hours. Most offices close for the day at 5:00 PM. The cleaning of the office can be done anytime after that.

In contrast, houses are cleaned in the daytime hours. If you are interested in starting your own house cleaning service…be sure to look at the downloaded, "Instant House Cleaning Kit" located at:

http://www.CleanUpTheProfits.com/homekit

If you have enough confidence in yourself to apply for a part-time job working for someone else, then you have what it takes, along with this information, to get your own office cleaning account that will earn you around $75 dollars an hour or more.

Many of the smaller types of offices that only want a cleaning service to come in and clean once or twice a week can provide you with at least $400 to $600 dollars or more every single month! You obviously wouldn't need many of these little gems to be making a full-time income from part-time work.

The larger offices or office buildings usually consist of different types of businesses or tenants under one roof, and they are generally handled by a property manager instead of an office manager. This larger type of account is usually cleaned Monday through Friday evenings each week and typically pays from two to three thousand dollars a month or more.

This larger type of account is usually an office building consisting of 2 or more floors. It sounds like more time-consuming work than it is. The amount of time it takes to actually do the routine office cleaning associated with the price range of $2000 dollars a month can easily be done by 2 people in 2 hours each evening.

Having only one of these 5 night a week accounts can instantly produce a $24,000 dollar a year income for you from only working part-time. Isn't that worth trying to get? You bet it is.

With only one or two accounts which are cleaned 5 evenings each week, you and one other person helping you, can realistically work only a couple hours each night and bring in 2 or 3 thousand dollars every month!

So, whether it's a big 5 night a week account or a smaller type of account that only gets cleaned once or twice a week...either type of account is well worth trying to get because it can earn you around $75 dollars an hour or more for your time and effort.

A significant benefit of this business is that you can pretty much come and go on your own schedule. There is no specific time that you have to start work, and you're off work on the weekends because all offices are generally closed then.

This Kit provides valuable information for anyone who wants to start their own office cleaning business.

For someone who already has an office cleaning business, this Kit will help you to expand your business and become even more professional. You really can work part-time and make a full-time income. You can at least clean offices part-time and make a tremendous amount of extra income. All you need is one account to get started, and you can get it.

You'll want all the small accounts you can get because they are very profitable. It all adds up and adds up fast. Just one customer will produce an immediate and ongoing monthly income for you.

Traditional advertising to get an office cleaning account is not very effective and is expensive. Use the material in this Kit to get customers for yourself. Now assuming that you have little or no money to spend for some cleaning supplies and equipment and you do not already own some kind of upright vacuum cleaner you are still ready to get started.

You don't need anything to submit a bid except the service agreement which is included in this Kit. Remember, you're not offering a product for sale, you are providing a service for sale at a price that makes it well worth doing.

Many people have started out using their own vehicle and $500 dollars for some equipment and supplies. I'll explain to you how to start with no money at all.

What kind of vehicle you have is not what they are going to be paying you for, is it? So make due and make it work. Put cleaning supplies in the trunk of your car or get permission to leave your cleaning supplies at their location.

There is usually some kind of janitorial closet around at each location. Get a monthly account lined up first and then concern yourself with getting what you need for your cleaning business. In this way, you are risking nothing, and you will know that your first monthly paying customer is ready and waiting.

Opportunities for you to obtain an office cleaning account are literally everywhere! Every town is full of small individual offices and a small one and two-story office buildings that need to be cleaned in the evenings on a regular basis. All you need right now is one of them.

7After you have submitted a few bids with the material in this Kit, your chances of landing your first account are excellent. It's a numbers game, and you control the numbers. At worst, you might submit 10 bids before you get one account, but it's still well worth it, because of the monthly repeat income.

You'll either get notified through the mail that you got the job, or your phone will ring and one of the office managers you gave the service agreement to, (the bid), would like you to start in a couple weeks or on the 1st of the month.

You'll always have a few days' notice before starting the job. When you do get your first office to clean, they don't expect you to start cleaning it on the day you put the bid in.

Even if you are hired right away, you'll usually have at least 2 weeks' notice before actually starting the job. Your initial objective is to be submitting those bids as often as possible and mail them a follow-up letter.

After you have put out a few bids and your first customer is all lined up, your income is going to be increasing, and more money will be coming in every month as soon as you start the job.

Always remember to get a copy of the key to the office and ask where they keep the toilet paper and paper towels for the restrooms. Also, write down an after-hours phone number contact for that office in case you need it.

After you get your first office cleaning account squared away, it's up to you to decide whether you want to do the routine office cleaning by yourself or have one or two people helping you. Although in the beginning, you should be on the job yourself even if you have 2 part-time people helping you do all the cleaning.

After all, that is your big selling point. The fact that you will be on the job. That is why you are in a position of doing better quality work than a larger cleaning company that sends in low paid help all the time.

It's a good idea to have some business cards made up at your local printer. You can get the minimum amount of black and white cards made up for around $30 dollars. Of course, you'll need to think of a name to call your cleaning service first.

Before you ever use up that first batch of business cards, you may very well have all the business you want from using the material I have given you in this Kit. So only order the minimum amount of inexpensive business cards.

Actually, you could just use your service agreement without having any business cards. After all, the bids will have your company name and phone number on them, just like a business card does. You'll also want to get some plain white envelopes with your company name in the upper left corner, use labels or you can just write that information in by hand.

The 2-page service agreement is your bid form. It is very professional in its appearance and detailed in its description of what is going to get done. Office managers like it very much, and they are impressed by it. The service agreement shows them that you are professional and it gets their attention.

hey, will only see it if you convince them to let you fill it out and give it to them. When getting started your primary objective is to submit bids, not to hand out business cards.

Remember, you're not paying for an expensive yellow page ad in the phone book. You have not rented an office for your service business because you don't need to. So consider the inexpensive cost of your bids to be a minimal advertising expense and give them out freely to office managers who are willing to look at your free estimate. One thing leads to another.

You have give out estimates (your service agreement) to get a job. You may get your first monthly customer after only putting out 3 or 4 bids. Even if you put out 10 or more bids before you get your first client, it will be well worth it, to lock into the monthly repeat income you'll receive from having only one office cleaning account.

Someone will hire you and your cleaning service, and you'll make good money every month from only working part-time. You'll also enjoy the independence of owning your own profitable service business.

So, have a few copies made of the service agreement and sales letters with your company name on them. This is very inexpensive to have done, especially if you can do it yourself on your own computer. All you need is a few of these service agreements for now.

Five or ten copies of your 2-page service agreement will get you started. By the time you submit these bids and mail your bid follow-up letter, you may have gotten your first account. You will at least have developed a lot more confidence in getting one, and you will now have more experience in estimating an office and submitting a bid.

What do you have to lose? A few copies of some bids is all you have on the line. Three or four bids could easily be submitted in one day, especially to the smaller offices like doctors' offices and real estate offices.

How to Begin with Little or no Money

The purpose of this information is to help you obtain a monthly office cleaning account of your own. A monthly account that will increase your present monthly income by hundreds of dollars or more and to help you develop a full-time income from only working part-time!

The methods explained in this Kit are practical, and they are geared towards someone with little to no money available. With no significant risk or investment, you can get your share of this profitable money-making service.

You may want your office cleaning service to grow big and have other people doing all of the cleaning for you, but for now, one customer is all you need to get started.

This information will help you to get a monthly office cleaning account and if necessary, to do it with no risk or investment. You'll soon learn how to price the job, submit the professional bid, and get the business. Remember, one monthly customer is all you are interested in at this point in time.

The focus of this information is aimed at getting you started and doing so rather quickly. The sooner, the better. The material in this Kit is condensed, direct, and to the point. Many people appreciate the quality of this useful information.

Learn how to get a profitable office cleaning account on your own and increase your income. My approach to getting started in this business requires little to no money, but it has proven itself to be effective.

If you wanted to own a restaurant, you would need a very large investment costing thousands of dollars. Then you would have to do some expensive advertising to get customers to come into your restaurant. In contrast, you can get started in your own office cleaning business with little to no money and after you get only one customer, you will have a guaranteed income coming in every month.

It makes no difference to your prospective customers where your office is located because they will never, under any circumstances have a reason to come to your office. So, you don't need to pay rent for some fancy office when your kitchen table will do just fine. In office cleaning, the business is getting the business.

This is what it all comes down to, and this is exactly what your Kit is all about. If you try to get business, you will get business. You will get a percentage of the bids that you submit. Even if that rate is low, that's alright, because as you know, just one office will be paying you month after month.

Build your Business with Small Offices

Big buildings or small offices? That is the question. Managing a few office cleaning accounts is easy. Only four or five small accounts could bring in anywhere from 40 to 50 thousand dollars a year or more, and you could have one person helping you do it all. You could also easily manage 2 part-time employees of yours who were doing all of the actual office cleaning for you.

When I speak of small offices, I am talking about offices that range in size from the smallest office in town, up to 10 thousand square feet in size. When you get into cleaning offices that are larger than 10 thousand square feet, you will most likely be looking at giant size office buildings in the area of 50 thousand square feet or more.

I have done them all, both big and small. In my opinion, the smaller, the better. For each individual hour of actual cleaning, the smaller offices are simply more profitable to be doing than the giant size buildings which are several stories tall.

If you want to take on the responsibility of cleaning large buildings (over 10,000 square feet), then you will have to have several part-time employees' working for you at one time. Around 50% of your monthly income will be spent on labor costs.

You would be doing a lot of managing, hiring, and firing part-time employees and continually looking for more customers, because you want to make more money. After a while, you may decide that getting really big and taking on large office buildings is exactly what you do want, but probably not. I don't recommend it. The big buildings are more trouble than they are worth.

The smaller offices are easier to manage, and they are more profitable to clean. In the long run, you will have a more secure business from small offices than from large office buildings. If you pursue small offices, rather than large buildings, you could still grow your business. There are plenty of small offices everywhere! Just look around and see for yourself.

I don't recommend growing too big in this business because the more accounts you take on, the more employees you must hire and the more problems you take on. The larger your business becomes, the more difficult it becomes to manage and to provide a quality service to your clients.

The quality of work that gets done by a smaller service business is usually better than the work that gets done by a larger service because the owner can be on the job when the work is getting done.

You can keep it simple and just specialize in routine office cleaning. Focus your energies on your routine office cleaning service rather than trying to juggle around several different types of services all at the same time. You don't have to provide an office with every kind of service available.

First, get better at the routine cleaning service and building your business, one office at a time. There are people who specialize in the other types of services, which are described in your 4 bonus reports.

Who are the Clients?

Who will pay you for your office cleaning service? Concentrate your efforts on contacting these prime prospects:

- New offices under construction
- Doctors' offices
- Dentists offices
- Medical facilities
- CPA offices
- Real estate offices
- Stockbrokers' offices
- Insurance company offices
- Daycare centers
- Banks
- Small office buildings
- <u>And much more</u>

You'll never see a doctor, a lawyer, a dentist, an insurance agent, a real estate broker, a banker or a CPA emptying the trash cans in their place of business. They just don't do it, but they have the money to pay to have it done, and that is exactly what they do. Their business is doing well, and they can afford to hire and pay for a private cleaning service to come into their office on a regular weekly basis.

Offices don't get that dirty in the first place because the so-called, "routine cleaning" is done on a regular basis. There are no beds to make and no refrigerators or ovens to clean. You don't do dishes either. Those things are not part of what an office cleaning service does.

Exactly what you do, is clearly spelled out in your service agreement so there is no misunderstanding. Offices are generally clean and air-conditioned working environments. You just need to keep them that way by maintaining their appearance on a regular weekly basis. Even the office restroom is not like cleaning some kind of dirty gas station restroom.

Each office will pay you every month because office cleaning is a monthly repeat service business. You only need to get an office to employ your cleaning service one time. After that, you will receive a monthly income from them as long as they are your customer.

The income you'll receive from having only one customer will continue month after month. Having only one office cleaning account, even a small one, can realistically produce several hundred dollars every month for you. Most likely, this will amount to several thousands of dollars, over the course of one year.

What About References?

References are a good thing to have, and they can be very helpful. Once you get your first customer lined up, then you will have a good commercial reference that you can use.

In the meantime, you should understand, that references are overrated. A typical office manager just wants a good cleaning service. If they are convinced that you will provide them with it, then that's all that matters to them. For now, you can simply write down 2 or 3 personal references and use them, just like you would on an employment application for a job.

Have them typed on a piece of paper, preferably on a so-called, "letterhead" with your company name on it. Make a few copies of it with the individual's names and phone numbers on it, so that the office manager can call them if they want to.

This issue of references won't always come up, but when it does, you will have something to give them. Honesty is the best policy. Simply tell them the truth. "You are just getting started."

After all, an honest and trustworthy cleaning service with the same people showing up, are the very qualities they are looking for. This is what they are most concerned about when they turn over a copy of the key to their office.

Your little office cleaning service is of greater value to an office manager than what the larger cleaning companies have to offer them. <u>You can do a better job!</u> The large cleaning companies will typically have a salesperson go into an office to submit a bid and try to convince the office manager to hire the company that he or she represents.

Then what happens is 2 or 3 (ever changing) minimum wage people show up by themselves to do the work and rush through the cleaning process. The office manager never sees that salesman again and the larger the cleaning company, the worse the cleaning is. The smaller the company, the better the cleaning is.

You can point this out and tell an office manager that you will personally be on the job. Experienced office managers do understand and appreciate this fact. This is also a big selling point for you and your cleaning service. It justifies your price is just as high as what the larger cleaning companies charge.

Many offices pay a lot of money for the cleaning to get done and they would much rather pay it to someone who is actually going to be there making sure it's getting done properly. Wouldn't you?

License and Insurance Information

When you are just starting out, a business license and insurance should be your only significant concerns. You will notice on the top of your service agreement, (the bid form) it says "licensed and insured." I wouldn't worry about it right now because you may not be doing any business yet.

You have put out a few bids, but you are not actually doing any work yet, and nobody has given you any money yet. You don't have the key to their office yet, and you are not actually cleaning it yet. You see what I'm saying?

You don't need a license or insurance to hand an office manager a bid with a price on it. However, a business license for a home-based cleaning service is very inexpensive, and it will keep you legal. Rarely if ever, will an office manager ask to see a copy of your insurance certificate and there is no reason to come up with one unless he or she is going to definitely be giving you the job.

So, shop around for the best deal for some insurance, but consider getting the job first. Get an income lined up first, then you can spend some money on insurance, cleaning supplies and equipment.

You can get started in this manner. If you are the one who is going to be given the monthly business on an account that will bring in several hundred dollars a month for you and the only thing standing in the way, is a copy of an insurance certificate.

Then put down the minimum amount of money required by the insurance company to get the policy in effect. You can then get a copy of the insurance certificate to give to the office manager and begin the work.

If you do not already have a business license, then go to your local courthouse and get one. Just tell the clerk that you want an occupational license for a janitorial service that you will be operating out of your home. There is a very minimal fee charged for obtaining this type of license. You can call your local courthouse and ask for the occupational license department. Find out exactly what the cost is and what you may need to bring with you.

When you are actually ready to get some insurance for your cleaning service, you don't want to buy more insurance than you need. There are big differences in the prices for this type of insurance. You must, therefore, tell the insurance agent on the phone, specifically what kind of insurance you want and compare prices.

In addition to that inexpensive business license from your local courthouse, the only type of insurance that you really need is what's called, "public liability and property damage." This is referred to as PL/PD coverage.

Depending on the insurance agent you are speaking with, they may call it something else, but it does not matter what they call it.

Put down the minimum amount of money needed to purchase the minimum amount of insurance coverage. You can then get copies of a small certificate of insurance that shows you have this coverage for your cleaning service. If and when a guaranteed customer wants proof of insurance, you will have it.

You don't need to be bonded to make money in the office cleaning business. City, County, and Government buildings require bonding, and quite often banks do also. However, the private sector of firms does not require bonding. When you are actually providing service to an account, a regular occupational business license and minimal amount of insurance are all you need.

When and if you want to know more about bonding, talk with an insurance agent specifically about what is called a "fidelity bond." This is an insurance policy that insures your clients against employee theft. Try to hire honest people in the first place when you need help, and you won't need any bonding.

If someone requires your cleaning service to be bonded and you would like to have that particular account, then add the cost of bonding onto the bid. Also, explain to them, that bonding doesn't cover anything without a criminal conviction taking place.

In other words, if an employee of yours steals anything of value while cleaning, then you would probably lose the account, with or without bonding because the customer would no longer trust the cleaning service.

I have been operating a commercial office cleaning service since 1992 without ever being bonded. Also, I have never once had to file an insurance claim for anything. The worst thing that may happen is you, or someone who is working with you knocks over a lamp or a photograph in a glass frame, and it breaks.

If this happens, you simply leave a note on the individual's desk and explain to them what happened and offer to replace or reimburse them for the item. You'll probably never hear from them about it. Once in a while, a minor accident happens, but usually, nothing is said about it.

So to review a bit, you do not need to be bonded to clean offices, so don't worry about it. It's just an extra expense you can live without. Very few offices will require that you are bonded.

Talk with different insurance companies about prices for that PL/PD insurance and about prices for bonding. Be sure to ask them, what minimum amount of money down is required, to obtain an insurance policy. If an office manager asks you who you have insurance with or asks you if you have insurance at all, you could tell them such and such a company, (the one you are planning on actually using).

Remember, the chances are that the office manager won't ask to see any proof of insurance or insurance certificate at all. Anyway, they don't need to, unless they are going to give you the job and they insist on seeing some proof of insurance. All you need to give them up front is the 2-page service agreement with your price on it and then be sure to mail them your bid follow-up letter.

One other thing you should be aware of is what is called "workers compensation insurance." Laws vary slightly from state to state regarding workers compensation. For example, in the State of Florida, a small business is not required to have it at all, unless they have 4 or more employees working for them. You can build yourself a very nice monthly income before you ever need to be paying for this type of insurance.

Regarding bookkeeping and records for your cleaning service, you don't need to be concerned about all that right now. When you need to be concerned about it, that will be a good problem to have. Talk to a bookkeeping service, a tax preparation service or accountant, and they will explain all of that to you.

They, of course, will offer to do that sort of thing for you, for a fee. When you actually need a bookkeeping service, you will be able to afford one from the monthly income coming in from your first office cleaning account, or you could learn to do it yourself. First...get a customer lined up and the guaranteed monthly income that comes with it.

The Best Part-Time Employees

Don't worry right now about finding someone to help you. Many people need a part-time job in the evenings. You will have time to find some help when you need it.

You'll know ahead of time when you will be expected to start servicing your first account, so you don't need a helper right now. You need an office cleaning account.

After spending lots of money over the years on help wanted ads in the newspaper and interviewing and hiring different types of people, I came to the following conclusion:

If you pay for just any kind of help wanted ad in your local newspaper you will attract a lot of people who are not really the best potential candidates for helping you to clean offices, unless you use the following phrase in your help wanted ad: " experience required" Believe me, that phrase in your ad weeds people out.

You will still get plenty of people calling in response to your ad, but the people who respond will be much better candidates for helping you.

Use your local weekly "Shopper or Penny Saver" type of newspaper. The one that most people get for free. A help wanted ad in this type of paper costs much less money than running a help wanted ad in your major daily newspaper. I have used them both and running a help wanted ad in the free paper will cost you much less money, and it will help you find the right person you are looking for.

You want a responsible person who is willing to work. Someone who really needs the money and who is responsible. Someone you can trust and feel comfortable with. It could be a retired person, homemaker or college student.

There is some good cleaning help to be found at your local college because some of these people are just entering the workforce and would actually appreciate a good part-time job that does not require them to work on the weekends.

You could also talk with the local employment office, but specifically request a homemaker, a college student or a retired person who has experience and would be suitable for doing this type of part-time work.

You can find a good cleaning helper without paying for a help wanted ad in the newspaper, but the newspaper will get you faster results. If you do pay for a help wanted ad in the paper, and you own an answering machine...when the ad actually comes out in the paper, you may want to temporally change the outgoing greeting message on your answering machine to give some details about the job.

For example, "Hello, you have reached ABC Cleaning Service. If you are calling about the help wanted ad"... now give some details and mention on your answering machine that, "you must have your own reliable transportation and we prefer someone who has experience in commercial cleaning."

This will weed out people even more and cause only very interested prospects to leave their name and phone number on your machine. Also, you won't even have to actually speak with all of those who call and leave their message for you, unless you want to return their call and talk with them.

You may already know someone who could use some extra income.

Ask them if they would help you clean your first account in the evenings when you get it. Make sure that you are aware of current hourly wages being offered by similar service businesses in your area. Your local Chamber of Commerce should have this information available for you.

Keep in mind that, companies who pay above-average wages are known as "employers of choice" and find it much easier to get and to keep, good part-time or full-time employees.

When you are ready to actually hire someone to help you, here is a valuable insider document that you should have them sign before starting to work for you.

On a blank sheet of paper or a company letterhead of yours, have the following short paragraph (on the next page), typed up and get your helpers signature on it.

This document you see on the next page will serve as a deterrent to any employee who is working for you from ever attempting to cause you any trouble if they happen to get involved in a car accident while working for you. It is not a legal document, but I have always used it without any problems occurring.

(Continue to next page)

(printed employees name here), hereby agree to assume all responsibility for the vehicle I am driving and any bodily harm which may occur while driving to or from accounts being cleaned by (your company name here).

SIGNED

DATED

Basic Cleaning Supplies

Cleaning supplies that you will need and use will cost very little. They represent a fraction of the cost of cleaning an office. The 2 cleaning liquids that you will use the most are all-purpose cleaner and glass cleaner in your own spray bottles.

Here is how you can turn your favorite bottle of all purpose cleaner such as (409 or Fantastic)... and... your favorite bottle of window cleaner such as (Windex) into A-FULL-GALLON... of super strenght cleaning solution! It works great and has been in use for many years in the commercial cleaning business.

ALL-PURPOSE CLEANER

Combine the ingredients below (in the amounts listed) into an empty one gallon container. Now... shake briefly and then add water to the top of the container.

Amount:	Ingredient:
1 qt.	Rubbing Alcohol
1 cup	Parsons lemon ammonia
1 teaspoon	Dishwashing liquid
16oz or 1 pint	Simple Green (optional)
21 oz.	Brand-name all-purpose (409 or Fantastic)

TOP OFF YOUR GALLON CONTAINER WITH WATER

Now...pour solution into a small spray bottle and your money saving all-purpose cleaner is ready to use!

Everyone likes this proven formula! The more you use, the more money you save!

GLASS CLEANER

Combine the ingredients below (in the amounts listed) into an empty one gallon container. Now... shake briefly and then add water to the top of the container.

Amount	Ingredient
1 qt.	Vinegar
1 cup	Parsons lemon ammonia
24 oz.	Brand name glass cleaner (Windex or other brand)

TOP OFF YOUR GALLON CONTAINER WITH WATER

Now...pour solution into a small spray bottle and your money saving glass cleaner is ready to use!

Everyone likes saving money when they can. With this formula, the more you use, the more money you will save. Even people who just clean their own home really like this money saving formula.

The other cleaning supplies that you will use a lot of is "Ajax or Comet" which you can purchase at most any store.

Your local janitorial supply store, listed in the yellow pages of your phone book, will be glad to sell you everything under the sun. However, I only purchase miscellaneous items like trash can liners, liquid stainless-steel cleaner, mop heads, spray bottles, etc. from the janitorial supply store.

It has been my experience that so-called "commercial cleaning products" don't live up to their name, only their price. There is really not a big difference in cleaning liquids. New cleaning products come out now and then, and you may want to try them.

Office managers don't know what you put into your spray bottles, and they don't care. You could do just fine using any general all-purpose cleaner and any glass cleaner from your local department store. It's up to you.

Note: if you are going to use a glass cleaner to clean any glass door that has solar film on it, (tinted glass) then be sure that your glass cleaner does not have ammonia in it as that would cause damage to the solar film. You should use a commercial "liquid stainless-steel cleaner" on stainless steel sinks.

The only place I've ever found the liquid stainless-steel cleaner is at a janitorial supply store, but this particular commercial product does work very well. You'll want to keep your cleaning liquids in small refillable spray bottles.

Quite often, each office will keep their own small trash can liners on site for you to use along with their paper products: toilet paper and folding paper towels.

You should have 2 different sizes of trash can liners: the small size, 24 by 33 inches and the large size, 40 by 48 inches, to empty trash cans into.

Most offices will pay for the small liners, and some offices will also pay for the large size liners and keep them at their place of business for you to use and some offices won't.

You only need to replace the small trash can liners when they start falling apart or have liquid spilled into them.

Note: You can rent equipment from janitorial supply houses like floor machines, wet/dry vacs, portable carpet cleaning machines, etc. If you are specializing in just providing the routine office cleaning service, (which is all you need to do), then you'll never need to use those things anyway. Someone else will.

If you have little or no money to buy any supplies or equipment for your cleaning company, then you have the following options to choose from:

1. You could possibly borrow the money from either a family member, a friend or a bank. They would feel secure about getting their money back because you will have already lined up your first customer and have a signed service agreement to prove it.

2. You could place a small classified ad in your local newspaper and find an investor who would be willing to loan you the so-called "venture capital."

   Five hundred dollars is not a lot of money to borrow. If you have to, offer to double someone's money. For example, you could offer to pay back a total of $1000 dollars over a 6 or 12-month period of time. Again, your collateral is the fact that you have the first customer already lined up.

   Paying back $1000 over several months won't be so hard to do if the account that you got brings in $1000 dollars or more every month.

3. Most janitorial supply companies will give you credit of $500 dollars or more.

They would most likely be more understanding than anyone else would. After all, if they help you to get started, then you will become a regular customer of theirs. If you already have that first customer lined up, they will be more inclined to help you out. Talk to them first. What do you have to lose?

The only actual machine that you will use on a regular basis is an upright vacuum cleaner. You may already own one of these, but it is a good idea to have a second one for backup purposes in case one of them is getting repaired. If you already have an upright vacuum cleaner than all you'll need is around...

$300 dollars for basic supplies and equipment. Later on, you can purchase a commercial upright vacuum cleaner. After many years of buying, and using different upright vacuum cleaners and paying for repairs that needed to be done, I can tell you that a good all-around commercial upright vacuum cleaner for your money is one called "Sanitaire" which is manufactured by the Eureka company.

You could also purchase a good used but reconditioned upright vacuum from a vacuum repair shop if necessary. Be sure to get a lightweight vacuum.

Basic Equipment List
(Needed for an office cleaning crew of 2 or 3 people)

- One upright vacuum cleaner with extra belts and a 50-foot extension cord.
- One 26-quart mop bucket with casters (wheels)
- One mop wringer for the mop bucket
- One large size cotton/rayon blended, mop head
- One commercial mop handle (gripper style)
- One commercial trash can (round shaped) with casters (wheels) (either a 32 gallon or 44- gallon container)
- One trash can caddy, (a tray to hold spray bottles) Or a commercial trash can apron, to hold bottles.
- One broom and dustpan
- One dust mop and handle for uncarpeted floor areas. (a dust mop is faster to use on hard service floors than a broom)
- One commercial (cone style) sanitary toilet bowl brush
- Three or more (1 quart) spray bottles and sprayer tops
- One case of small trash can liners (24 by 33)
- One case of large (40 by 48) trash bags to use in the commercial trash can with wheels.
- One dozen or more terry cloth rags
-

The Routine Cleaning

When you are just getting started, your cleaning crew will consist of you and one or two additional people. Everyone should always work as quickly as possible from start to finish.

You and your help should always begin working in a circular pattern once you enter the office. Begin the routine cleaning at the entrance area and work in a clockwork pattern.

Work around the perimeter of the office. Don't hop around all over the office going from one area and over to another area and another desk. Things will get overlooked and missed that way. Work in a circular pattern following the perimeter of the office in a clockwork motion.

Stick to a plan when you enter the office of who is specifically cleaning what. For example, one person will be dusting and emptying the trash cans while another person will be vacuuming and also cleaning the front door. Have a plan of who is cleaning what before you actually show up to clean the office.

The routine cleaning that takes place in every office is pretty much exactly the same thing that gets done in every office. The front page of your service agreement (included in this Kit) describes the details of the cleaning to be done. However, the nightly routine office cleaning, basically always consists of the following simple routine:

1. The trash cans get emptied. (only change the liners if need be)
2. Dust the cleared areas only, of desks, tops of file cabinets and shelves, using a feather duster or a rag.
3. Vacuum the carpet
4. Sweep and mop the uncarpeted floor areas.
5. Clean the bathrooms and refill the paper products.
6. Clean the front door and sweep the outside entrance area.

One person should wheel around the commercial trash can with large trash bag liners in it and go from desk to desk, emptying the small trash cans and doing the dusting as needed.

Another person can go right to work on the other areas to be cleaned. Plan your work, divide up the cleaning tasks, and always work in a circular pattern. **Note:** If you are interested in how to start your own house cleaning business be sure to look at:

http://www.CleanUpTheProfits.com/homekit

How to Correctly Figure the Bill for the Month

In any type of service business, what you charge is always based on what the market will bear. No two cleaning services will come up with the exact same price when estimating a job and submitting a bid.

You don't want to bid a job at too high of a price because you will not be in the competitive ballpark with other cleaning services. However, you can, and you should charge enough to make it worthwhile and keep your business profitable. Don't hesitate to put in a lucrative bid.

There will be some accounts where you end up making less than expected, but here and there you will get one that earns you more than expected, and things will even-out for you. In other words, a more profitable account will help to compensate a less profitable account.

When you have come up with a price that you feel confident about, then fill in the price on the service agreement and give it to the decision maker. **Do it in person, face to face. Don't mail it in.**

You will gain experience in estimating with the very first job you get. You'll know exactly how long it takes to clean that office and you can use that office as a guide when bidding future accounts.

You don't want or need to be the lowest price bidder to get the job, if you are, you will regret it. Experienced office managers do not base their choice of cleaning services on who gives them the lowest price. Some of them do, but most of them do not.

An office manager who is accepting estimates will typically look at 3 bids and go with the middle of the road priced cleaning service. If you spend time trying to underbid your competitors, then you would just be contributing to poor quality work because you would not have enough money to pay good wages to your help and make a healthy profit for yourself.

The fact is, if you are not charging enough money to do the job properly, then you won't spend the time and make the effort it takes to do a good job, and you would not even want to continue doing it.

However, I assure you that, it is well worth doing and it is typical to find yourself in a position where you are earning $70 to $75 dollars an hour or more for your time and effort to do the simple routine office cleaning.

Experienced office managers know that you get what you pay for from this type of service business. Most of them want a good job done, and they know that they won't get it from the lowest priced cleaning service. They already have learned this from experience.

When you apply for any kind of a job, (outside of office cleaning accounts) you have to try and convince the employer to hire you. You try to convince them that you really want the job, and that you would be right for the position. This same effort is what you need to do with an office manager. Simply try to convince the office manager to hire you and your cleaning service, based on the quality of service. Based on doing a good job. Not based on a low price.

I have been hired many times to provide office cleaning service, instead of a lower priced competitor, simply from using the professional material I have given you in this Kit. The introduction letter, the professional service agreement (the bid), the bid-follow up letter and the reminder letter will convince an office manager to hire you and your cleaning service, more than the price that you give them.

First of all, you should understand that there are different ways and things to consider when figuring the price for a bid. The way I'm going to explain to you is simple, easy, and accurate. You should have an understanding of this:

"The time it takes to clean," **versus**, "the price per cleaning."

With or without considering the following information, the square foot estimating chart in this Kit will be an easy guide for to use. You don't charge an hourly rate to clean offices. You should always bid your work "by the job" to make a decent profit. Always, price it at "so much money per cleaning," not by the hour.

Shoot for a minimum of $70 dollars an hour or more for a 2-person cleaning team. You can charge this much, and you can get it. The office managers have no idea how long it takes for you to clean their office and they don't care. You should always consider the price based on at least 2 people doing the cleaning. You could do it by yourself, but it would take much longer to do.

Even on the smallest office in town that gets cleaned only once a week and may only take 30 minutes to clean, you should still, have a minimum charge of at least $70 to $75 dollars per cleaning. As a rule of thumb, one person can do the complete routine cleaning on 2200 square feet of floor area in approximately one hour.

However, you should always think in terms of a 2-person cleaning team when you are pricing the job. So, 2200 square feet can be cleaned by 2 people in 30 minutes, instead of one hour. This would be a small office but in this example, $70 to $75 dollars <u>or more,</u> would be an appropriate "price per cleaning."

A 4400-square foot office would take 2 people approximately one hour to do the routine cleaning. An appropriate "price per cleaning" in this example would be about $80 to $85 dollars <u>or more,</u> as pointed out on the square foot estimating chart.

Any office that is medically related in any way should always be priced 25% higher because they require more time-consuming work. For example, a medical office has treatment rooms in it, and each treatment room has a sink in it. Add 25% more for medical.

NOTE: Medical offices have a few trash cans in them with a red colored trash can liner. These trash cans are considered to be what is called "hazardous material," and you are not required to empty them at all. An entirely different service does that, and not the cleaning service.

If you are estimating an office that has approximately 6600 square feet, then using a hand-held calculator, divide 2200 into 6600. Your answer is 3 hours. Now divide that in half, because 2 people will be doing the cleaning. 3 hours divided by 2, equals 1.5 hours.

It will take 2 people about 1 hour and 30 minutes to clean this office. If you are shooting for $70 to $75 dollars an hour or more, than this "price per cleaning" would be about $105 to $110 dollars, as pointed out on your square foot estimating chart.

The point is that you should consider and be aware of how long it will take to do the cleaning because of the hourly wages you will be paying to your helpers. Another little rule of thumb that you should consider is this: most offices have 2 restrooms in them. If the office has more than 2 toilets in it, then this would justify increasing your price for each additional restroom.

Also, a 5000-square foot medical office will have treatment rooms in it, and most every treatment room has a stainless-steel sink in it, to be cleaned. In contrast, a 5000-square foot real estate office will not have any treatment rooms with sinks in them, so you could make your "price per cleaning" on the lower side but add 25% more for medical offices.

Your square foot estimating chart is an excellent guide for you to use, but if there are more than 2 toilets in the office or if they want anything done in addition to what is listed on your service agreement, then you would be justified in adjusting the price upward.

You would want to increase your price because of the additional time involved in doing the work.

So, how do you figure the bill for the month? First, you determine what you want your individual "price per cleaning" to be.

Then you do this:

Example #1: The office you are giving an estimate to, is only going to get cleaned once a week, at $70 dollars a cleaning. Now, multiply that weekly amount of $70 dollars times 52 (weeks), and you come up with a total annual amount of $3,640 dollars. Now, divide that annual amount of $3,640 dollars by 12 (months). The answer is $303.34 per month. This is how to do it.

This is the correct way of doing it. It is also very logical and justified. If you figure the monthly bill in any other manner, you would be shortchanging yourself, and you would also have to be changing their statement periodically over a 12-month period of time. This is the very fair and correct way to do it.

Example #2: The office you are giving an estimate to, is going to get cleaned twice a week at $85 dollars a cleaning. Now multiply that weekly amount, which in this example is $170 dollars (because it is cleaned twice a week) times 52 (weeks), and you come up with a total annual amount of $8,840 dollars. Now, divide that annual amount of $8,840 dollars by 12 (months). The answer is $736 dollars per month.

Example #3: The office you are giving an estimate to, is going to get cleaned three times a week at $115 dollars a cleaning. Now multiply that weekly amount, which in this example is $345 dollars (because it is cleaned three times a week) times 52 (weeks), and you come up with a total annual amount of $17,940 dollars. Now, divide that annual amount of $17,940 dollars by 12 (months). The answer is $1495 dollars per month.

This line of reasoning, along with your square foot estimating chart will serve you well, up to around 10,000 square feet. Beyond that, you would be looking at much larger office buildings. Large buildings that are over 10,000 square feet in size are typically a 2 or 5 story building which may be 50,000 square feet in size.

They are always cleaned 5 nights a week, and they are priced in an entirely different manner. Usually, the monthly price of large buildings is based on a price such as 10 cents a square foot to arrive at the total monthly price. However, as I mentioned before, the small offices and small office buildings are simply more profitable per individual cleaning and much easier to manage.

Always ask the office manager if they know what the square footage of the office is. If they don't know what it is, then simply estimate it by pacing off the rooms and hallways or just walk around the perimeter on the outside of the building. A close estimate of the total square footage will be close enough.

Remember...the square foot estimating chart in this Kit is an excellent guide for you to use. However, it represents prices that you would never need to go below.

The prices could be raised higher, and you may do that depending on what the customer wants to be done. Are there more than 2 restrooms? Does the customer want anything done that is not already spelled out on the first page of the 2-page service agreement? You can adjust your price higher if need be, but you don't need to lower it at all.

The Best Time to Bill the Office

Every office out there gets cleaned on some kind of regular basis. Usually, it gets cleaned either 1,2, 3, OR 5 evenings each week. I recommend putting in your bill once every 2 weeks unless you or they prefer it to be put in on a once a month basis to simplify things.

Put your bill in on the 1st and on the 16th of every month.

You can mail it in, but for quicker results, I always put the bill in an envelope on the desk of the individual who takes care of it. It gets processed much faster that way. Do it in the evening while the cleaning is being done.

Whether you have 1 or 10 part-time employees, you can tell them that payday is on the 10th and on the 25th of each month. This will give you some time to receive your check in the mail and deposit it into your business checking account.

Note: the next few pages consist of:

"A sample bill" - (A)
"An introduction letter"- (B)

"A professional service agreement (the bid)" This is a 2-page document. (C & D)

"Bid follow-up letter"- (E)
"Reminder letter" - (F)

Please note that throughout these letters and documents, you will notice the name "ABC Office Cleaning." You will need to retype the following documents in "Word" with your own company name and phone number on them. Just start typing the 2-page service agreement, and the bid follow-up letter as these are the documents you will need to get started with.

Your typing will allow you to choose the font size you like and also to add any color you may prefer to your own company name, etc. Note: The first sentence of the introduction letter (B) should be removed if you are mailing this letter to offices without first speaking with someone in person or over the phone.

A Sample Bill

(A)

ABC OFFICE CLEANING Licensed & Insured

Date:

To: ABC Office 101 Suite Life Blvd. Your Town
U.S.A.

DESCRIPTION OF CHARGE: AMOUNT:

INTERIOR ROUTINE CLEANING $648.00

TOTAL AMOUNT DUE: $648.00

(6% sales tax if applicable) $38.88

TOTAL $686.88

(B) **The Introduction Letter is on the next page**

ABC OFFICE CLEANING
Licensed & Insured

Thank you for the time and hospitality given to me as we discussed your janitorial arrangements. **ABC Office Cleaning** provides routine office cleaning on a nightly basis. <u>Extra service</u> is provided for such things as cleaning interior and exterior areas of entrance doors, also, spot cleaning of carpet and glass, disinfecting the telephones and wiping fingerprints from around light switches.

Every week, furniture is vacuumed as need be. Picture frames and the tops of file cabinets are dusted, and doors are wiped for fingerprints. These are just a few of the typically overlooked or neglected areas by most janitorial services.

ABC Office Cleaning strives to go the extra mile so you will be pleased with our cleaning service and the quality of our work. Our price is guaranteed for at least one (1) full year, and please be assured that our bid is submitted to do <u>the entire job</u> every night.

We do not cut corners or rush through the cleaning process. We take pride in our reputation, and our quality of work reflects this. We have the ability to bring into your office the personnel, and equipment necessary to be absolutely certain that whatever cleaning task needs to be done, is done on time, without compromise.

Please keep us on file, as we would very much like to be considered for this position. I am confident that we can establish a beneficial and lasting relationship with your firm.

ABC Office Cleaning's service agreement is based solely on performance on your behalf, and you will surely <u>see the difference</u> in your office. I look forward to hearing from you.

Sincerely,

ABC Office Cleaning

    Your name, mailing address, and phone number go here

        (introduction letter ends here)

A Professional Service Agreement

(C and D)

ABC OFFICE CLEANING
Licensed & Insured

Janitorial Service Agreement DATE

This is a janitorial estimate prepared for the office of:

Routine interior cleaning nights per week

THE QUALITY OF CLEANING STANDARDS WE ADHERE TO:

1. Control floor appearance by vacuuming and or sweeping.
2. Mop hard surface floors
3. Dust and clean horizontal surfaces (cleared surfaces of desks, chairs, tables, filing cabinets, furniture, and unobstructed work areas)
4. Sanitize telephones.
5. Empty waste receptacles and damp wipe if needed.
6. Remove smudges around door jambs, push plates, light switches, glass partitions, counters and unobstructed work areas.
7. Sanitize and polish all water fountains.
8. Restrooms: Thoroughly clean and mop with a germicide. Clean mirrors, partitions, urinals, toilets, and sinks using disinfectant/detergents. Refilling of soap and paper products will be performed with supplies furnished by your firm.
9. Remove soil on entrance door frames, handles, glass, and threshold.
10. Sweep surface of immediate exterior entry areas.
11. Leave offices and furniture in a neat, orderly fashion.
12. Report any unusual occurrences, malfunctions or damages.

(Put your mailing address and phone number contact here)

PRICE QUOTATION
(D)

The following price is good ninety (90) days from the date on this agreement. After that time has expired, the price will need to be reevaluated.

TOTAL COST PER MONTH (INCLUDING SALES TAX IF APPLICABLE):

$

Description of Cleaning:

Special Instructions (if applicable):

We do not claim perfection, but we promise pride, quality and perseverance. Since you are not bound to any contract, our only security is your day to day satisfaction. You will be pleased with the difference a professional service can make in the appearance and cleanliness of your office.

I _____, authorize **ABC Office Cleaning**, to begin

janitorial service of our office on the following date:

(Put your mailing address and phone number contact here)

(Note: the service agreement is 2 pages)

Bid Follow-Up Letter

(E)

ABC OFFICE CLEANING
Licensed & Insured

Thank you for the time and hospitality given to me as we discussed your janitorial needs. I was pleased to submit my proposal to you, and I am confident that we could establish a beneficial and lasting relationship.

Let me take this time to point out certain special routines developed by **ABC Office Cleaning**. As stated in the service agreement, the routine cleaning is done on a nightly basis, <u>but extra service is provided</u> for such things as cleaning interior and exterior areas of entrance doors.

Spot cleaning of carpet and glass. Disinfecting the telephones and wiping fingerprints from around light switches. Every week, picture frames and tops of file cabinets are dusted, and doors are wiped for fingerprints.

These areas are usually overlooked or entirely neglected by most janitorial services. We strive to do the small things so you will be pleased with our cleaning service, and our price is guaranteed for at least one (1) full year. Be assured that we have bid to do <u>the entire job</u> every night.

If we are not selected as your cleaning service at this time, then I hope things work out well for you with the cleaning service you have chosen.

In any event, please keep me on file, as I would still like to be considered for this position at a future time.

My service agreement is based solely on performance on your behalf, and <u>you will see the difference</u> in your office if we are given the opportunity to clean it.

                                              Sincerely,

                                              ABC Office Cleaning Your name
                                              goes here

(Put your mailing address and phone number contact here)

Reminder Letter

(F)

ABC OFFICE CLEANING
Licensed & Insured

We would like to remind you of <u>the quality of cleaning</u> that you are missing by not utilizing our service. We not only provide the cleanliness you desire in your office, but also the reliability, trust, and thoughtfulness you expect from your own employees.

Our office cleaning service is supervised, and all work is provided professionally. Our only objective is to please you with the quality of our service. <u>We do more for you</u> than what is expected of a typical cleaning service.

ABC Office Cleaning provides the most complete office cleaning service available, and once a company accepts our proposal, they are more than pleased with our performance. We would like to add your business to our family of satisfied customers.

Sincerely,

ABC Office Cleaning

Your name goes here

(Put your mailing address and phone number contact here)

Square Foot Estimating Chart

Square Footage Price Per Cleaning

0 to 3000 $70 to $75

3000 to 4000 $75 to $80

4000 to 4500 $80 to $85

4500 to 5000 $85 to $90

5000 to 5500 $90 to $95

5500 to 6000 $95 to $100

6000 to 6500 $100 to $105

6500 to 7000 $105 to $110

7000 to 7500 $110 to $115

7500 to 8000 $115 to $120

8000 to 8500 $120 to $125

8500 to 9000 $125 to $130

9000 to 9500 $130 to $135

9500 to 10,000 $135 to $140

These prices reflect the least amount you should charge for your cleaning service, not the highest amount you may be able to charge a customer.

Labor Time / Estimate Guide

Consider Your Time and Labor Cost When You Price The Job

In the office cleaning, and residential cleaning business, a rule of thumb can be used to determine a price for cleaning. This rule of thumb is the foundation for remaining profitable.

A cleaning crew usually consist of 2 or 3 people who are doing the work. If you are paying your employee $10 dollars an hour and you determine it will take 2 people two hours to do the work, then you should at least double your labor costs to make a good profit from your cleaning service. In this example, your labor cost would come to $40 dollars so you would charge at least $80.dollars to the customer.

The same amount of work needs to get done by either you alone or by a crew of 2 or 3 people so you should still price it the same way. If you stay in the cleaning business long enough, you will eventually have a crew of individuals working for you.

The routine cleaning performed in 2200 square feet of office space can be done by 2 people in 30 minutes or by 1 person in one hour. Knowing this time factor by itself will always keep your price competitive and in the right ballpark.

Once you determine the approximate time, it will take to be cleaned and by how many people, you can then decide what your labor cost will be to get it cleaned.

Always double your labor costs, and you can't go wrong. Your price will be more accurate, competitive and profitable.

Labor Time / Estimate Guide

(Rule of Thumb for a Full Cleaning)

2200 square feet of routine cleaning can be done by 2 people in 30 minutes or by one person in one hour. Use this rule of thumb to figure out what your labor cost will be. Note: you can't always cut the time in half by adding one additional person. It won't work out that way. The following figures are very accurate and will keep you on track to determine your labor cost.

4400 square ft. cleaned by 2 people = 1 hour 4400 square ft. cleaned by 3 people = 40 min.

8800 square ft. cleaned by 2 people = 2 hours
8800 square ft. cleaned by 3 people = 1 hour and 20 min.

17,600 square ft. cleaned by 2 people = 4 hours
17.600 square ft. cleaned by 3 people = 2 hours and 40 min.

35,200 square ft. cleaned by 2 people = 8 hours

35,200 square ft. cleaned by 3 people = 5 hours and 50 min.
35,200 square ft. cleaned by 4 people = 3 hours and 30 min.

70.400 square ft. cleaned by 3 people = 10 hours and 30 min. 70,400 square ft. cleaned by 4 people = 7 hours
70,400 square ft. cleaned by 5 people = 4 hours and 30 min.

Remember…on office cleaning accounts that want service 5 times a week you should present them with 2 different price scenarios. One for a full cleaning 5 times a week and another price for a light cleaning/full cleaning schedule in which a full cleaning would get done two times a week and a light cleaning would get done 3 times a week.

Accounts that get done 5 times a week really don't need to have a full cleaning done every night. It is up to the customer, but a light cleaning/full cleaning schedule will be appealing to them because it will save them money.

On the nights that a light cleaning is done, it takes about half the time (or less) than a full cleaning would take to get done.

Once you determine your individual price per cleaning, you should reduce It by half on the light cleaning nights. On 5 night a week accounts there is an average of 22 cleaning nights in a month.

Divide 22 into the monthly estimate to determine the individual price per cleaning and cut it in half for the light cleaning nights.

In this example, you would then add up 3 nights at the full cleaning price Plus…2 nights at the light cleaning price to get the correct weekly amount.

Then multiply the weekly amount by 52 weeks (for the year) and then divide by 12 (months) to get the correct monthly amount for the customer.

The Business is "Getting the Business."

Before pursuing efforts to obtain customers, it seems appropriate that you have an understanding of the nature of this business. In the section that follows, we get into the various ways, "Proven Methods of Getting Customers," but first, let's talk about the business in general.

The best way to get an account is the direct approach. By going direct, I mean either calling to speak with an office manager, mailing an introduction letter to them or simply walking into the nearest office in person.

Either way, it costs you nothing at all, and you have nothing to lose but a 2-page service agreement. You don't need to be a fast-talking salesman. They are not hiring a salesman but a service, to clean their office properly. If you try this direct approach of walking in off the street, just dress nicely and try to convince the office manager to hire you and your cleaning service.

Understand, that you accomplish this, by first getting them to allow you to give them an estimate using your 2-page service agreement. That's the goal, but as far as convincing them to hire you and your cleaning service, it's not rocket science. You would have to make the same kind of effort to get a part-time job at a fast food joint working for minimum wage.

Remember, you're not always trying to get a new customer. After you get 1 to 4 customers, you may not even want anymore.

Sometimes you make contact with an office manager who currently has a cleaning service that is doing a very good job for them. Usually, that is not the case because there are more bad cleaning services out there than good ones.

In any event, regarding the direct approach of contacting office managers, you would simply say the following: "Hello, my name is John Doe with ABC Cleaning. "Could I speak with the office manager?" Now, even if they say to you that they already have a cleaning service, you would still say to them that, you would like to submit a competitive office cleaning bid for them to keep on file. (Get their reaction).

If they are agreeable to it, then take a quick walk around the office and look at it. Walk around briefly, look in the restrooms and fill out the bid. Also, ask them if they know what the square foot size of their office is. Your objective is to submit a bid as often as possible and mail a bid follow-up letter.

If they are not interested in looking at your service agreement at the time, then they are probably a waste of time. Go to the next office manager.

There are hundreds of offices all around you. You really only need a few of them to be making a good living from the part-time evening hours.

Basically, what is taking place, in a nutshell, is this: you are out to convince an individual office manager to let you and your cleaning service be the one to: <u>empty the trash cans, clean the restrooms, do the dusting, and vacuum the carpet.</u>

This individual office manager needs to be convinced that it is better to have you and your service clean it for them, rather than someone else. They need to come to the decision that your service is better or different than the other cleaning companies who may have called on them in the last month.

They are already convinced that it needs to be done and they are probably already paying every month to have it done. They usually have learned from experience, that they get what they pay for and they are already happy with the cleaning service that they have now or they are not satisfied with it.

Remember, you don't need to be the lowest bidder in town to get the job. They will hire you and your cleaning service, based on the quality of service they think they are going to get, not on a low-priced bid.

Especially if they are not happy with the service, they have now. If that is the case, then they are very willing to pay more money for a better job. The decision to hire you and your cleaning service is made before you ever actually clean the office.

You can convince them to make this decision and hire you, simply by using the phone script, the sales letters, the service agreement and the various methods for getting customers, explained in this Kit.

So what is the difference between 2 people who both own a cleaning service and both do a good job of cleaning, yet one of them brings in $25 thousand dollars a year, and the other one brings in $200 thousand dollars a year?

The difference is in the ongoing mixture of marketing methods that is or is not taking place. In this type of service business, persistence prevails, when all else fails. If you are after one monthly account or 100 monthly accounts, the key to getting them is the same. The following methods are the least expensive and the most effective ways to start, operate and market your own office cleaning service.

The Best Proven Methods for Getting Customers

Any kind of advertising or marketing that you may do serves as your billboard, your attention getter, so to speak. Advertising shows those people who want and need your service, where to find you. It makes them aware of you and your service and directs them to you.

Any type of advertising that you do is for the specific purpose of capturing the attention of office managers who are interested in hiring you and your cleaning service.

In today's world, there will always be other cleaning services similar to yours, so the type of marketing that you do helps to distinguish you from your competition.

The type of marketing that you do enables you to stand out from the crowd and be noticed.

Marketing is the process of selling something. It is not a one-shot deal, like running an ad in the newspaper for one day or doing a one-time mailing to a group of 500 people and expecting your phone to ring off the wall. Marketing your office cleaning service doesn't work that way.

You have an office cleaning service to sell, and office managers are the only ones who are buying it. You want to be in the right place at the right time, and your persistent marketing methods are done on a regular basis, cause that to happen.

Your marketing efforts must involve ongoing regular activities which are directed towards these "office managers" for the specific purpose of getting customers. The majority of promotion is in the motion. This is the key to getting customers. In other words, the ongoing activities you do and the regular efforts you make to market or promote your cleaning service is the key to getting a new monthly account.

Target the Office Managers

The marketing of your office cleaning service consists of "the ongoing efforts you make to promote your business." This is the process of selling your service. These efforts must be directed towards specific individuals who are office managers and in some cases property managers.

Your marketing efforts in general, should not be directed towards the general public, as the case is, with a radio, newspaper or TV advertisement.

These traditional forms of advertising are not half as effective for office cleaning as the other methods explained in this Kit.

In addition to working the methods in this Kit, if you still want to spend some money on a traditional form of advertising and you can afford to do it, then place a small classified ad or a small display ad in a local weekly newspaper for at least three full months or more. It needs to be in the newspaper for a lengthy period of time for it to produce results for you. Put an ad on Craigslist for your area right now.

Unlike a radio or TV advertisement, people can look at the internet at their own convenience. When they are ready to go online, your ad will be there. Many different types of people will see your ad and eventually it will make its way to the attention of an office manager. Consider a one-page website but only place ads for it that are for your geographical area.

You should use capital letters in bold print so that it is more noticeable and stands out from the other ads. What should it say?

OFFICE CLEANING SERVICE FOR HIRE
FREE ESTIMATE

(Your company name & phone number)

That's all a newspaper ad would need to say. Your phone won't ring off the wall, so don't expect it to because your newspaper ad is attempting to reach office managers only and not the general public. However, if you get only one office cleaning account as a result of your newspaper ad, it would be money well spent because of the repeat income every month.

This should not be your first choice in methods used to obtain customers because of the expense involved in continuing to run this ad. Your first choice should be more directly targeted to office managers.

Your direct contacts with office managers can be made, through the mail, over the phone or in person. By understanding who your targeted audience is, your marketing efforts will be more economical and effective.

Now, in regards to contacting office managers directly over the phone. Before you say "hold the phone, Sam," I'm not doing any phone

solicitation. You should understand that direct phone contact is just one of several different ways of getting customers and you should at least understand this one method because it is very effective. It is used by large franchised janitorial companies, and it can be used by you too.

Experts say that the response from 100 telephone calls is similar to the response from 1000 pieces of mail. Making direct contacts by telephone gives you faster results than if you were driving all over town. Local phone calls cost you less and get you feedback much faster.

Office managers and receptionists are receptive to this type of phone call. It's not like you are calling to try and sell them encyclopedias or something like that. They already know that their office must be cleaned and many of them are not happy with the quality of cleaning they are getting. When I first started my own office cleaning service back in 1992, I got my first customer because of a direct contact made from a phone call.

The following phone script guideline is based on experience and actual phone calls to offices. It is an excellent guide to use regarding this particular method, whether you make the phone calls yourself or someone else does it for you.

PHONE SCRIPT GUIDELINES

You will be talking to either:

1. A receptionist
2. The office manager
3. A property manager

Hello, my name is may I speak with the office

manager?

Typical responses: You say:
Yes, hold on, How do you pronounce (his or her) last name?

What is this in reference to? I'm with (ABC Office Cleaning) and
I'd like to speak with (him or her) about submitting a competitive bid for you to keep on file. Things change.

| We already have a cleaning service. | I understand. I thought that you might, but I would still like to speak with (him or her) about submitting a competitive bid for you to keep on file. Things change. |

When you do get through to the decision maker, you say:

Hello (Mr. or Miss) ; My name is

. I'm with (your company name) here in (your city). The reason I'm calling you, (Their Name) is I would like to submit a competitive office cleaning bid for you to keep on file. Are you satisfied with the quality of cleaning being done?

THE 3 SECOND TEST

This 3-second test works like a charm to convince almost any office manager, (at least 1 out of 4) that they have been wasting their money every month on a bad cleaning service and need to make a change. Here is how you can prove it to them. In the lobby area of any office, you will notice on the walls, "picture frames, photo's, college degrees, paintings, etc."

Simply take your fingers or a rag and wipe along the top edge of one of these items on the wall. Do this in front of the office manager or receptionist and 9 out of 10 times you will find an inch of dust on your fingers which is very noticeable and plain to see.

This little demonstration is very impressive at convincing anyone that the cleaning service they have at the moment is a waste of money because they are simply not dusting the office, the way they should be.

This 3-second test by itself is a real icebreaker and will cause them to be open-minded and receptive to accepting you and your service agreement on the spot.

RAISE YOUR PRICE

When you do get to actually submit a bid, keep your price up, don't lower it. In the office cleaning business, the lowest bidder is not always the one who gets the job. Usually, they are the ones who do not get it. Not only will you make more money by charging more, but you will have a better chance at getting the job, so price it right, to begin with.

A higher priced bid is not only more profitable, but it separates you from the crowd and implies that your service is better and deserves a higher price. So, don't be the lowest priced bidder, you'll regret it if you are.

You will get a monthly office cleaning account because of the impression you make on a particular individual office manager. It's you, your letters, your service agreement and your persistence that will influence any office manager you come into contact with.

VISIT POTENTIAL CUSTOMERS IN PERSON

Even if you operate entirely through the mail with professional letters, your potential customers still like to see the face behind the business. It's more personable, and it adds more influence to whatever letter you use.

A personal visit or an occasional phone call also helps to convey friendliness and builds confidence in you and your company from the office managers perspective.

On the flip side, you should keep in mind that, there is a face behind every office and office building. <u>The decision maker.</u> This is the only one, you are trying to influence.

You must make contact with these specific individuals. Remember, you want to be in the right place at the right time. Keeping in touch on a regular basis with the right people causes that to happen. Simply talking with the right people and keeping in touch with them is the best way to build your service business.

You should still mail your introduction letter and other items on a regular basis. It's all part of your overall marketing strategy. Don't view this as a chore, but a challenge. To a great extent, being in the right place at the right time is a numbers game. The more you tell, the more you sell. The squeaky wheel gets the oil. You understand what I mean?

The more bids you put out, the more business you will get. Anyway, other types of advertising are very expensive and not nearly as effective as dealing directly with office and building managers. These are the decision makers.

Increase the number of contacts you make, one at a time. Develop a list of names, addresses, and phone numbers of individual office managers who do employ a private cleaning service in your area. Keep in touch with these people and your income will increase as a result.

Generally speaking, the more office managers you contact, the more likely you are to find people to do business with. The more you keep in touch with them, the more likely you are to find people to hire you and your cleaning service.

Spend some time visiting office managers in person, face to face. You could walk in off the street (have a service agreement with you) or just stop in to see the people you have already mailed a letter to. If you do walk in off the street, be sure to get one of their business cards while you are there, to add to your own mailing list information.

If they employ a larger cleaning service that sends in their cleaning people to do the work, then the owner of the cleaning service is not even on the job. There is not any employee of any cleaning company who cares as much as the owner of the cleaning company does, about the quality of work being done.

This is what gives you a real opportunity to submit a bid and get the job. So count on your personal visits or direct phone calls to get your business started, but your consistent mailing program to a targeted list will most often be the key that opens the doors and should not be neglected. How often should you mail something to the same office? At least once every 2 months is good.

TURN YOUR BUSINESS CARD INTO A MINI-BROCHURE

Your little business card is an excellent marketing tool in itself. When an office manager is ready to call you, they will most likely look for your business card, so make the most of it. Think of all that wasted space on the back of your business card. Why not use it to list your special services, a slogan or mention a free estimate?

An inexpensive way to have a message on the back of your business card is to have a rubber stamp made up and then do it yourself. Here's an example:

WE DON'T CUT CORNERS

WE CLEAN THEM

FREE ESTIMATE

Carry some business cards with you at all times and get a business card from every contact you make, so that you can add that information to your growing mailing list. Whenever you are speaking to an office manager in person, one reason for giving them your business card is so you can get their business card in return.

Develop your own mailing list and never leave it up to those you want to talk with again to call you. You just can't depend on that. You must always take the initiative. It pays off in repeat monthly income, so be persistent.

RESEARCH

Once each week, you can, and you should, look at the business section of your local newspaper and look for articles about new offices that will be opening up or new managers who just got promoted. Recently issued business licenses are also published in the newspaper as are building permits. If it is the type of business that may employ an office cleaning service, then give them a call and find out about it.

Whenever you are driving around town, always look for a new building or office that is under construction and make contact right away.

Get on the phone like a private investigator and find out who you need to talk with about the janitorial arrangements. Send them an introduction letter, then call them back about submitting a bid.

PROMOTE WITH POSTCARD MESSAGES

Many people underestimate the power of a postcard. A postcard message conveys a sense of urgency to your potential customer. An attractive, eye-catching postcard gets your message out in the open where everyone can see it. Use some color on it instead of just black and white.

You could also put an eye-catching graphic on it of someone cleaning. Many printing shops have a book of free graphic art or so-called "clip art" that you could choose from. Best of all, the postage on a postcard costs less than a regular stamp, and your postcard "reminder message" will contribute very much to your marketing efforts. A postcard message keeps your name out there and accomplishes your objective of, keeping in touch.

You can purchase blank postcards at your local post office with the postage already on the cards. This is a direct and economical marketing tool. Use one or all of the following <u>3 postcard messages</u> on a regular basis. You can write or type these messages on the postcards, or have a local printer do it all for you.

A FRIENDLY REMINDER

(your company name here) not only provides the cleanliness you desire in your office, but also the reliability and trust you expect from your own employees. We look forward to hearing from you,

(your company name and number here)

A FRIENDLY REMINDER

(your company name here) provides the most complete office cleaning service available. Once a company accepts our proposal, they are more than pleased with our performance. We look forward to hearing from you,

(your company name and number here)

A FRIENDLY REMINDER

(your company name here) strives to do the little details so you will be pleased with our cleaning service and the quality of our work. We would like to add your company to our family of satisfied customers. We look forward to hearing from you,

(your company name and number here)

BID APPEARANCE

You know that old saying "a book is judged by its cover "? Well to a large extent, that situation applies here. An office manager who has 3 bids sitting on his or her desk has a decision to make. As mentioned earlier, they usually rule out the lowest priced one, but my point here is that, if your bid looks professional to them, then they are influenced by this. Your service agreement is a reflection of you and your cleaning company in the eyes of an office manager.

Put your 2-page service agreement into a presentation folder. Even an inexpensive folder with a transparent cover will do just fine. These folders are available at any office supply store. It's a little professional touch that carries a lot of weight.

You and your bid will be taken more seriously, and it shows how important it is to you. It just leaves them with a very professional impression of you and your cleaning service, regardless of what the price of your estimate is.

You won't get a second chance to make a first impression in regards to your service agreement, so make the most of it and put it into a folder. Make this little extra effort, and your service business will simply look more professional to an office manager, and that is exactly how you want your service business to be perceived by them.

Prepare 5 or more bids ahead of time and have them ready to put out. You can type in the information on the service agreement, or you can write it by hand. Either way is alright, but hand it to the office manager or decision maker in person, instead of mailing it or faxing it to them.

TALK ABOUT THE PRICE

You have walked through the office, and you have decided what the price should be. Now, before you put the price on the bid, go ahead and ask the office manager or building manager what they are paying now to have it done.

They may or may not be willing to tell you what that price is, but you can still ask. Are they willing to pay more for a better job? What particular problem do they have now with the current cleaning service?

You would not want to make the same mistake as them. Quite often, they will answer these questions for you, if you simply ask them. Of course, some people are not willing to discuss anything about their current cleaning service, they just want an estimate from you, and that's all, so give it to them and leave it at that.

In any event, talk to them about the price range that you have in mind just to get their reaction to it before you put the actual price on the bid.

They may be willing to pay more than you had in mind, but they just want to pay it to a cleaning service that will do a better job for them than what they have now. Their response to your questions can give you valuable insight that your competitors don't have because they didn't ask.

Square foot figures are a guide for you to go by, but you may want to take into consideration the individual circumstances. They may have been paying the same price each month for the last 2 years, and that's what they think it's worth.

They may be on a tight budget and only have so much money to spend on the office cleaning each month. They may be generous in their attitude toward the cleaning service and willing to pay top dollar for a job well done.

In reality, you charge what you can get, and you get what the market will bear. You will increase your chances of getting the job if they are willing to openly discuss their honest opinion of the price before you put it down in writing on the bid. Sometimes they will and sometimes not. Either way, you will further your knowledge and experience in estimating and in dealing with office managers.

BE CONSISTENT

Research has proven that an advertising message must be repeated to be remembered. Don't expect your phone to ring off the wall from doing just one mailing. It just doesn't work that way. To promote a service business by mail, you need to send a variety of mailings on a regular basis to the same people.

Your objective is to be in front of the potential customer when the need arises. To be in the right place at the right time. So, use a variety of direct mail promotion on a regular basis.

Start accumulating your own mailing list (one by one) of specific individuals in your area who employ a private cleaning service. You could collect the business cards of these office managers, or you could simply type a list of these people in your computer and save it.

Either way would be just fine. Start mailing to them every 2 or 3 months and personalize your mailing with an individual's name on it. Don't just mail something to "ABC Office" or to the attention of "office manager." You want to get past the receptionist and get your message to the decision maker, so be sure and write down the correct person's name on the office business card or in your computer records.

This direct mailing method is efficient, and very economical compared to other forms of advertising. Your advertising dollars are well spent when you deal direct. Communicating your company's message is an ongoing process, but along the way, you will develop a secure customer base of repeat business.

Office cleaning accounts are acquired one at a time, so stick with it. Persistence is power. Getting a potential customer to remember your cleaning service is the best way to attract them. Getting them to want the cleaning service that only you can provide them with, is the ultimate goal.

POSSIBLY DO SUB-CONTRACT WORK FOR ANOTHER CLEANING COMPANY

This is an excellent way of getting started in this business which is largely overlooked. You could contact some of the larger more established janitorial companies in your area about doing sub-contract work for them. Offer to take over the responsibility of cleaning one or more of their monthly accounts for them.

You would make less money than you would if it were your own account, but many large cleaning companies participate in this sub-contract arrangement because they are simply too busy. Quite often they will pay a sub-contractor to take over an account rather than hire another part-time hourly paid employee.

Explain to them that you are just getting started and have a business card ready to give them. It could be well worth your time when you are just starting out and provide you with an excellent reference to use when submitting your own bids.

CONSIDER GETTING A SALES PERSON TO HELP YOU

Getting the business is a job in itself. One creative way of doing this that might appeal to you is to work with a salesperson and offer to pay them a 10% commission. They would receive this 10 percent every month as a residual income on any monthly account they help you get. This would cost much less than splitting the profits with a partner.

This is a bit easier said than done because most salespeople want a salary plus a commission which is typically taking place with the big janitorial companies. There are, however, many people who would be agreeable to this arrangement and they could work on it at their own convenience.

There is room to play within the price range of these monthly accounts, and you would actually be creating an opportunity for someone else to make money every month. You could also involve more than one individual in this arrangement if you wanted to.

In any event, this salesperson would most likely put their efforts into making phone calls for you and giving you the name and location of an office that wants an estimate. You would always have the final say so on the monthly price.

This salesperson could also contribute names and addresses to your mailing list, but they should only be from people they have actually spoken with on the phone. Whatever they do, if it results in you getting an account, they should get credit for it.

It would be worth paying them their monthly commission from it. You can find retired people to work on this commission only situation. However, you should not depend on them to build your business for you. Depend on yourself and the efforts that you make.

If you do pursue the help of salespeople who are not working for a salary, you could use the "**COMPANY / SALESPERSON AGREEMENT**" (on the following page). It should be signed by the salesperson. You could make changes in it if you want to, but I suggest using it as it is.

COMPANY / SALESPERSON AGREEMENT

This agreement is between <u>(YOUR COMPANY NAME)</u> hereafter referred to as "the company" and <u>(THE SALES PERSONS NAME)</u> hereafter referred to as " the salesperson." In return for contacts made by the salesperson and bids submitted by the company as a result of the salesperson's efforts: (for the purpose of securing monthly office cleaning accounts for the company) the salesperson will be compensated as follows:

A. (80% of the first month's gross revenue) on each individual account secured as a result of the salesperson's efforts will be divided up and paid to the salesperson in three equal payments during the first three months in which the cleaning service is performed at such location.

B. Beginning on the 4th month in which service is performed by the company and every month thereafter, the salesperson will receive 10% of the gross monthly income from the account or accounts in which the salesperson was involved in securing for the company and will be paid such amount by the company on a monthly basis.

NOTE: If one or more of the monthly accounts secured as a result of the salesperson's efforts, opens up or expands to an additional location which is also serviced by the company, then the salesperson will again be compensated as described in both **(A)** and **(B)** above. If the account simply relocates to a new location then only **(B)** listed above, will apply and remain in effect. **(A)** Will apply only to the increased monthly amount if applicable. All compensation listed above will become null and void if, for whatever reason, the company is no longer servicing the account(s). If for whatever reason, all or part of the companies accounts and or business is sold, then the salesperson will be paid a final (one time) flat fee of 10% of the dollar value of the sales price that the accounts secured by the salesperson contributed to the total selling price of the business. Such figure would have to be determined at that time based on the actual sales price of the business and the dollar value that each individual account contributed to the total sales price. A non-competitive agreement shall exist between the company and the salesperson for a period of 3 years from the date in which the most recent bid was submitted by the company or by the salesperson on behalf of the company. During such time, the salesperson agrees not to compete with the company through ownership or involvement in an office cleaning or janitorial type of service business in the area of: (YOUR CITY AND TOWN). The salesperson will have knowledge of private and confidential information regarding the amount of money the company is being paid to service a particular account or accounts and agrees in good faith to protect the privacy of the company and not use or share such confidential information in any way that would be detrimental to the company.

The salesperson must have helped to secure at least one account for the company within one year from the date of this Agreement, or this agreement will become null and void.

Signed and dated on

Company name
Salesperson

BULK MAILINGS

Another way of dealing with or developing your own prime mailing list would be to mail a large batch of your letters at one time. Speed up your marketing efforts by purchasing a list of doctors in your area on adhesive mailing labels.

Check with your local newspaper marketing department about purchasing such a list. Ask about other lists they may have available but start off with doctors' offices.

Your local tax collector's office can also furnish you with good lists of professionals in your area. Mail an initial batch of letters to people on this list, then follow-up by calling everyone on your list. When you call them, personalize your bulk mailing list with each decision makers name for possible future mailings. Cross off the unreceptive ones and remove them from your list.

Zero in on your targeted group of people who are worth keeping on your mailing list. If you use this method, I recommend mailing out _only_ 10 to 50 letters at a time and then giving them a phone call. Always follow up.

Whichever way you develop your mailing list, one at a time or sifting through a large batch of mailings for the best ones, I assure you that it sounds more involved than it actually is.

When you have developed a good list of only 100 targeted people that you are maintaining contact with through regular mailings such as letters, postcards, and an occasional phone call, it will lead to submitting bids, and your business will increase as a result of it.

Remember, only a handful of monthly office cleaning accounts can make a world of difference in your monthly income and maybe all the business you want to handle.

FAX A FULL-PAGE AD

Here is another method of keeping in touch with office managers that can help get your business off the ground. You know by now that you should always be developing your own good list of names and addresses of offices and office managers. Put this information on index cards or on your computer but be sure to collect the actual business cards from each potential client along with their office fax number.

Imagine being able to afford a full-page advertisement for your office cleaning service in your local community. Wouldn't that be great? Well, you can afford it and here's how. It's not in a magazine, a newspaper or the phone book, but it is a full-page ad, and office managers will see it.

Fax machines are a marvel of modern office technology. Every office has a fax machine, and if your message gets faxed, it gets noticed. The trick is doing it on a regular basis to get results.

Have one side of a full-side sheet of white paper typeset at a local printer or do it yourself in "Word" on your own computer. You just want it to look the way a flyer or a full-page ad would normally look.

I suggest starting off your full-page fax message with a large bold headline at the top of the page in the form of a question. Here are 3 good examples:

WHO'S CLEANING YOUR OFFICE TONIGHT?

**IS YOUR OFFICE CLEANED BY PEOPLE DOING
DETAILED PROFESSIONAL WORK?**

**ARE YOU GETTING A COMPLETE FIRST CLASS
OFFICE CLEANING SERVICE?**

You don't have to say much in your fax page ad. It's not about what you are saying but what you are doing. You are keeping in touch and reminding them about you and your cleaning service. Be sure to emphasize the statement "FREE ESTIMATE" near the end of the page with your company name and phone number on it.

As soon as you get your first office cleaning account or if you already have one, like a doctor's office for example, then you could fax a message to similar types of offices and mention in your fax page ad that "Dr. Will B. Good" recommends ABC Office Cleaning (your company name) because their office is cleaned by people who care about doing detailed professional work.

Keep on reminding the specific offices, on a regular basis, by faxing them your full-page ad. Gradually start building your own list of local fax line phone numbers to go along with the mailing list information you are developing.

Sometimes the fax number is listed in the Yellow Page ads in the phone book, and the fax number is usually always located on the office business card.

Most of the time you would simply need to call the individual local offices that you are interested in and ask them for their fax number over the phone. They are usually very willing to give it out. If any explanation is necessary on your part, then simply state that you own a service business and would like to send them information about it. You can fax local messages for free on your own fax machine, or you can go to a local printer and fax a batch at a time for a minimal fee.

NETWORKING

There have been entire books written on the subject of networking, and I am not going to overwhelm you with this subject matter. Instead, I am going to simplify and explain it in terms of how it applies to getting office cleaning accounts.

Networking is really very simple to do. It starts off by you contacting anyone with any kind of service business, other than one like yours. These people have some kind of a service business with customers who have offices. These are the individuals who you would be networking with to help you get customers for your office cleaning service business.

Networking can be explained by giving you an actual example:

If John Doe owns a carpet cleaning service and does any type of commercial carpet cleaning, then he is in contact with offices. You would simply call or visit John Doe. Introduce yourself and give him one of your business cards and get his.

Explain to him that you are just getting started and trying to get customers for yourself. When you come into contact with the need for carpet cleaning to be done, you could recommend him for the job if he comes up with a potential customer for your cleaning service.

In doing so, you could both be helping each other to get more business. Even if you only hear from John once in a while about an office cleaning account, that would be great, and it would have taken place because of networking.

You could network with several different companies at the same time. One little-known service to network with is a local courier service. This type of service offers same day delivery of letters and small packages from office to office. Almost every day, a courier service with important documents or packages stops into an office to make their delivery. You can find them in your phone book or from searching online. Other overlooked services to network with are those that deliver coffee, water or snacks to offices.

The best services to be networking with are the 4 types of service businesses which are described in the 4 bonus reports located at the end of this kit. Networking is an underrated but effective way of getting a new business off the ground. Make contacts with people who make contact with offices or who work for offices. One thing leads to another and networking can help both, your business and the other persons business.

The Key to Success in Your Own Cleaning Business

Small business makes a big difference in America! Did you know that small businesses provide about half of all the private sector jobs in the United States?

Much of the hope for the job market rests in the hands of small business owners just like you. You're in good company so stay immune to obstacles, especially rejection. Don't let it stop you at all.

Change the way you look at rejection, and it will modify the way you run your cleaning business. Whenever someone says they're not interested in your cleaning service, let it fuel your competitive side. It may not be today or even next month, but you can work on a strategy that will turn a "No" into "Yes." You can embrace rejection competitively.

Many people have a business idea they think will make them money. They seem to think that the idea by itself will make them rich. That's not the way business actually works at all. It's about the day to day nuts and bolts of your idea.

Trying to be better at it and different than anyone else is a good game plan. Success in your own cleaning business is the result of good planning. Not good luck. You can get your business started. You can get new customers, and you can succeed in your own cleaning business! Follow through, work on your business and above all, be persistent.

You don't have to convince people that cleaning needs to be done. They already know that. You want to persuade them to employ your cleaning service and pay you well for it. You want to be perceived by the customer as professional because that is what they prefer in a cleaning service. Contact them about helping them instead of selling them.

Don't come across as needy for the work but as someone who is helpful. Someone who can solve their problems and offer a better solution than what they have had in the past.

You can do it. Use the information in this Kit to get started. Start a top 10 list and gather information such as the customer's name, address and phone number.

Then keep in touch with them about your cleaning service every 30 days. No other form of advertising is more effective and cost so little as a direct approach to the decision maker consisting of phone calls, letters, and greeting cards.

Use them to promote your cleaning business to potential customers, and it will pay off for you in a growing business. Small businesses provide about half of the private sector jobs in the United States and have accounted for about 65 percent of total job creation in the past two decades.

So much hope for the job market rests in the hands of small business owners. Small businesses make a big difference! That's you, and you're in good company, So don't let rejection stop you and don't be afraid of it ... "embrace it."

This will change the way you look at life and the way you run your cleaning business. Whenever someone says they're not interested in working with you or your cleaning service, (for whatever reason) let it fuel your competitive side Many people have a business idea they think will make them money.

They think that the idea by itself will make them rich. That's not the way business actually works at all. It's about the day to day, nuts, and bolts. Try to be better and different than any other cleaning service in town.

A well-known baseball player from long ago named "Babe Ruth" is famous for hitting so many home runs. What is not well known is that he struck out many times more often than he hit home runs. My point is...whenever you speak with a decision maker about your cleaning service, it's like stepping up to the plate.

Keep trying, and you'll get your share of home runs too. It may not be today or next month, but when you keep trying, you can turn "NO" into "YES. "When getting a "YES" from a new customer becomes more exciting than the opportunity itself, you can embrace rejection in a competitive way that is good for your business.

You can get your cleaning business started. You can get customers, and you can be successful! Follow through with potential customers, work on promoting your business and be persistent about it. A mindset of persistence and an attitude of embracing rejection is essential to success in the house cleaning business.

Creative Bidding Method Gets More Accounts

The following information explains a priceless, and proven method you can use to get paid top dollar for your cleaning services. Literally more money than your original estimate.

Most people in their own service business never take advantage of this information because they just don't know about it. By the time you finish reading, you will have the expertise you need to join the ranks of the highest paid and most professional service business owners in the world. Regardless of how big or small your business is at this time, you can make more money using the information that follows.

Only after 20 years in my own service business did I finally discover and fine tune this clever estimating method. It then became crystal clear to me; just how powerful this method is getting paid more money than expected.

Getting paid a higher price than your estimate has never been easier. It's a win, win situation too. Use this method, and you'll get paid much more money than you expected. You and your new customer will both be happy.

After figuring out this estimating and bidding strategy, I went on to test it and use it with great success. It has enabled me to earn thousands of dollars more from my office cleaning business than I would ever have earned without using the method.

Now... you can do it too. Read the following information and let it sink in. There is a bit of psychology to this method, but I am going to explain it to you, so it is very simple and easy to use. You don't need to be a salesperson either.

You'll know exactly what to do and what to say, I assure you. with "this proven method." What is it and how does it work? Well, once you understand it you will see just how easy it is for you to use and how effective it is at getting a top dollar price for your cleaning service. I will begin with a real-life example so you will have a better understanding of the method.

Price, Bid and Estimate for Maximum Profits...

If you have ever walked into a pawn shop anywhere in America with anything of value to sell, the person behind the counter in the pawn shop will always ask one question of you first. The question is, "how much do you want for it"?

They always ask that question first, and the reason they do that is to get the item you have at the lowest possible price. By asking you "how much do you want for it" they are feeling you out, so to speak.

They are getting inside your head in an attempt to find out how low of a price you are willing to accept for your item. If the price you give them is low enough, they will agree to it on the spot. If the price you give them is too high, they will tell you, "they can't go that high for it."

The point is, by asking you that question first, they involve you in the decision as to what the final price will be. The price that you will be paid for the item of value that you have to sell.

It always works out to their advantage, and that is why they always ask that question. It helps them to get the item of value that you have at the lowest possible price from you and to do it with your help. By the way, if you are ever in that situation and getting asked the question, "how much do you want for it "... answer them with... "as much as I can get. A million dollars would be nice. "

Now that technique of asking a question to help determine a price is referred to as an involvement device, and it works very well in different situations.

When it comes to the pricing, the bidding, and/ or the estimating of an office cleaning account, that example (above) works in reverse and it works great. Your cleaning service is of value to you and of value to your customer.

You want to be paid the highest price that you can get for your cleaning service, and you should be, but how do you get it? How do you know what price the customer is willing to pay you for your cleaning service? You want to attempt to find that out because if you don't, you quite often will be shortchanging yourself by hundreds of dollars a month. Here is what to do:

First, you determine the price as you normally would. If you already have your own way of doing that and you are happy with it, that is fine.

If you don't already have a way of figuring out a price to charge for your cleaning service, then I recommend the **Instant Office Cleaning Kit** or the **Instant House Cleaning Kit.** These kits are exactly what you need to get started.

Located at: http://www.CleanUpTheProfits.com

Note: The majority of the time, most cleaning customers will hire one cleaning service over another, not based only on price but based on the individual who is giving them that price and providing the cleaning service to them.

The decision as to what the price is going to be is just as important as who is going to provide the cleaning service itself. The customer will hire the cleaning service they are most comfortable with. The one they feel is going to do a good job for them. The one they think is professional and trustworthy.

It is important to know this because most people who pay for a private cleaning service (commercial or residential) are well off financially, especially commercial cleaning customers. They can afford to pay for a job well done, and they are willing to do just that.

However, when you figure out your price as you normally would and then just tell them what it will cost them for the cleaning service without any discussion taking place, here is what always happens next.

You just showed them your hand. You just told them, how low of a price you are willing to do the work for. You may think that your price is not low, but they may think it is low. The price that you figured may be a good price to get, but you usually can always get paid more, when you use this method before telling them that you are willing to do the work for such and such a price. Remember who you are talking to. If they think that your

price is low, they are not going to argue with you about it. They will not tell you to charge more money even if they are willing to pay more money to you for your service.

This is where the method comes into play. It will always work out to your advantage, and that is why you should always use it. The method will help you to get the highest possible price for your cleaning service and to do it with their help.

You will not look like you don't know what to charge because you do know. Remember, you have already figured out a price. Do your best at doing that because that price you figured out, maybe the price that you get paid but now...by putting the following method into use, you will get a substantially higher price for your service most all of the time.

The Profit Range Factor Explained

Anytime you're in a situation with someone who wants the service that you have to offer them, you are in a great position to make money, but how much? Here is how to make the most of it. There is a big difference between selling a tangible product like a TV set, compared to selling a service.

The selling of a tangible product is a one-shot deal, and the work is done. However, the selling and buying of a cleaning service consist of work that is going to be done over and over again.

It is important that your customer has looked at your service agreement and understands exactly what your cleaning service will actually do for them.

Your service agreement should already point out the details of the service that your company will be providing them with, so they realize exactly what they are going to get for their money and that it is money well spent.

You want and need their cooperation, and you want them to see things your way...to understand your perspective and agree with you on the value of your service. Associating your price...with the quality of the service you are going to provide to the customer go hand in hand.

In other words, justifying a higher price with a better and more detailed quality of service is very reasonable and makes sense.

It is a common practice of many successful service business owners to pad the price for their service to have room to work with. Many times, you will find that the decision maker is in total agreement with you on the higher price that you point out to them. You just won't know unless you bring it up and talk about it.

Always ask, "what was it about the previous service that was not getting done properly." It is logical and reasonable for most people to be willing to pay more for a better job to be done. After all, if they were so happy with the cleaning service they had, they would not be talking with you now.

Also, keep in mind that you are not speaking with the potential customer to make new friends with them. You need to remain somewhat distant and businesslike when you are discussing your service business.

It is important that you and your customer consider the fact that the price you get paid for your cleaning service will have a domino effect. To understand that is to see the big picture.

The big picture is the fact that the price affects everything and everyone associated with your cleaning service. That includes the quality of work that gets done. The customer is in their own business to make money. They make a good profit and can afford to pay for a private cleaning service. You should make a good profit too, and they know it.

The ideal customer for you to have is someone who is willing to pay you enough money to make a good profit for yourself. Enough money for you to pay your help very well.

Enough money to keep you happy and motivated to do a good job for them on a regular basis. It is in the best interest of both you and your customer.

The fact is, a smart decision maker (the customer) is someone who would want you to be in that position of getting paid well for your cleaning service.

If the person who hires you and your cleaning service is a reasonable person, they already know it is in their best interest if you are paid well, and you do make a good profit from them. After all, they want you to provide them with a good quality of service.

They expect good work to be done and they know it won't happen if the job is priced too low. They can afford to pay for a private cleaning service, or they would not be talking with you about it.

The long-term quality of the cleaning service is directly related to the price you get paid. Most decision makers already know this fact. However, the biggest mistake that many cleaning service owners make is not charging enough money for their service.

Don't underestimate the value of your cleaning service. If you act desperate to get the job and just tell them a low price in an attempt to get hired, you will not only look unprofessional to the customer, but you will regret it.

All that approach would do is set you up to be taken advantage of. You don't ever have to do it that way. There is a much better approach explained to you in this e-book. Project a confident professional image, and it will pay off for you. The fact is, the customer will never have a good cleaning service unless they pay a good price for the work to be done.

They might as well start by paying it to you. Remember, one good customer (a profitable one) is better than having 2 low priced customers.

Getting paid extra money to work with and to work for is a quality driven price that works out best for both you and the customer. An excellent customer will pay it to you. That's what this information is about. Getting outstanding customers for your cleaning service who pay you a top dollar price. You can get them!

The following page is a simple one-page chart that is called a "price range chart." You can re-create it in "Word" on your computer, print it out, or you can simply draw it out on a sheet of paper with a pen and a ruler.

Either one would work just fine. Make a few copies of it, and you will have what you need with you when you are ready to discuss the price for your cleaning service with any customer.

Remember, you would first determine a specific dollar amount for an individual cleaning. The price you expect to be paid for your cleaning service.

ALWAYS engage the decision maker in a brief conversation regarding the price to get their feedback on it. After all, the final decision as to exactly how much money is going to be paid for the cleaning service is up to them. After you figure out a price to clean an <u>office,</u> a <u>building</u> or a <u>home,</u> what you should say to the decision maker is this:

"There is a price range that buildings this size could be cleaned for. That price range is anywhere from $ XXXX... to…$XXXX.

$ XXXX." Always look them in the eye and say this with confidence because it is true.

Now see the price range chart on the next page

The first space for a price (the lower line) is where you will have already put in the price that you have determined. On the price range chart below, your price for an individual cleaning will go on the line next to the lower dollar sign $.

Now, next to the upper dollar sign $ on the price range chart put in a price that is 50 percent higher than the lower price. I always put in a 50 percent higher price on the price range chart at the top of the chart next to the upper dollar sign.

NOTE: Do this, even if you think that the increased price is high. They may not think it is high at all or they may have already been paying it to a previous service and are willing to pay it to you.

The "price range chart" (on the next page) is a visual aid to use along with questions that you should always ask. First, determine an initial base price to use as a starting point on the lower line of the chart on the next page.

The Ultimate Chart That Does the Selling for You

Price Range Chart

HIGH

R $_____ **per cleaning**

A

N

G

E $_____ **per cleaning**

LOW

Here's Exactly What to Say for Great Results

You have a visual picture and a price range for the customer to look at. Now get their reaction to it. Remember, you have already filled in your 2 prices on the" Price Range Chart, "and all you need to do with it is show it to the decision maker and ask questions. Just show it to them, and they will react to it.

Now... ask them 3 questions to go along with the chart as they are looking at it.

1. Does this seem reasonable to you?

2. Is this price range in your budget?

3. Would you like the cleaning service to be responsible for changing the burned-out ceiling lights?

Changing burned out ceiling lights is not a standard part of any cleaning service. It is not something you have to do but rather something you may offer to do. You can use it as a bargaining chip, and it will help the decision maker to justify paying a higher price.

Remember, the customer's decision to hire you or not hire you is not all about the price. It is more about trust and confidence. It is about whom the decision maker is most comfortable with giving the office key to.

Even if you are not really confident in yourself, then act like you are. If you appear to be confident in yourself and in your cleaning business, they will be much more inclined to put their confidence in you too.

Openly discussing the price with the decision maker is an opportunity for you to earn their trust and confidence because it shows them that you know what you are talking about. This will work in your favor. You may only have one chance to speak about the price and the quality of your cleaning service, so make the most of it.

Use your power of observation and read the person and their reaction. This will be easy to do because you have used the price range chart, and the questions as tools to open up the customer and find out what they think about the price.

They may already have been paying a higher price for some other cleaning service. They may be unhappy with the quality of the service they are used to getting and are already willing to pay more for a better cleaning service. Either way, proceed with your brief discussion and come to an agreement.

It is better to aim high and miss than to aim low and make it. If you try to build your business around a cheap group of clients, you will get them and regret it.

Based on their feedback and their reaction, use your best judgment to decide on the final price that you will put on your service agreement. They may think that your higher price on the top of the chart is very reasonable.

If so, that is the price it will be. The higher price. The more profitable price. You should always try to take the lead. If their response is a positive one, then just go with the higher price and ask them when they would like the new service to begin?

It would always be in your best interest to have a few profitable customers rather than a bunch of low-priced customers. With this information, you can now get the good clients. The profitable customers are the best ones to have, and you can get them.

Even if they don't agree to the higher price, they will most likely agree to a price that is higher than your original estimate that is written in at the lower end of the chart. This is because you involved them in the decision as to the price they are going to pay instead of just telling them what price you are going to charge.

There is a big difference. You have also given them a visual aid to look at with the "Price Range Chart." You are not pulling prices out of the air. You know what you are talking about and the price range chart says that to them loud and clear.

It is also the truth. If you were to get 3 or more estimates for a cleaning service, each one of them would be a different price. They may be close, but they would all be different. It's not necessary for a customer to do that now that they are talking with you. They will conclude that fact on their own.

The customers who pay for a cleaning service are also different from each other. It is important to consider that fact before giving someone a price to do the cleaning.

Some people are more reasonable than others. Factor that difference into your price and it will always be right on the money; right where it should be. You factor that in by talking with them. By engaging the decision maker in a brief discussion to get a feel for that individual customer.

Discussing your price with the decision maker in this way makes a world of difference in the outcome of the price. Simply by handing them that "price range chart" to look at and asking a couple of questions, you now involve them in the price "decision-making process."

It really works out best this way because the customer has a choice to make and a decision to make regarding the cleaning service. It's a big decision and an important one too. They want to get it right just like you. They want to make the right decision. Now you are actually helping them to make that decision. This way, you can both take part in that process.

Also, keep in mind that your attitude is important in determining the successful agreement that you and the decision maker come to. Do not be negative and self-critical about the value of your cleaning service or it will be visible to the customer.

You are in business to make money. Your cleaning service is valuable, and you should be treated with respect and well paid. You will be when you take this information to heart and do what you learn from this e-book.

Attitude by itself makes a big difference between those who become very successful in business and those who do not.

I have seen many times when a person's low self-esteem translates into a low price for their service. You don't get a second chance at making a first impression, so make it a good one.

When you are talking with the decision maker about the price, think positively and be confident in what you say. Many times, a customer will want to do business with you simply because their perception of you is that of a confident professional. People like to do business with someone who they think is professional.

By the time you finish reading this information, you will have the expertise you need to join the ranks of the highest paid and most professional service business owners in the world.

Regardless of how big or small your business is at this time, you can make more money than what you had in mind with your original estimate. Getting paid a higher price than your estimate has never been easier. It's a win, win situation too. Use this method, and you'll get paid more money than you expected. You and your new customer will both be happy.

After figuring out this estimating and bidding strategy, I went on to test it and use it with great success. It has enabled me to earn thousands of dollars more from my office cleaning business than I would ever have earned without using the method.

Now... you can do it too. Read the following information and let it sink in. There is a bit of psychology to this method, but I am going to explain it to you, so it is very simple and easy to use. You don't need to be a salesperson either. You'll know exactly what to do and what to say, I assure you.

When you are talking with the decision maker about the price, think positively and be confident in what you say. Many times, a customer will want to do business with you simply because their perception of you is that of a confident professional. People like to do business with someone who they think is professional.

Use the information in this e-book, and you will be professional. You will get paid like one too!

Remember, your cleaning service is of value. It is of value to you and also to them. The customer is usually a business owner or the manager of a business, but the customer does not own a cleaning service like you do. They are not in the cleaning business, but they are going to pay for one. They don't know what the price range is until you show it to them and tell them about it. They will be glad you did and so will you because it works.

Word for Word Interviews with Office Managers

I had recorded many conversations with decision makers so I could improve my method of bidding. I have put the best 3 together for you to learn from. These 3 are perfect examples for you to follow. These conversations took place with 3 different office managers at 3 different offices over a period of time. Each resulted in my bid being accepted.

Read each one, and you will understand how a successful bidding process should be conducted. Each office was different, but basically, the technique I used was the same. You will hear the questions that I asked and how I handled each situation. This is the best way for you to learn how to speak with an office manager when submitting your bid. It is just like being there yourself.

So, come along with me and let's get a new account. Notice the questions that I ask are always the same, but the answers are different. Also <u>remember...after</u> every bid, you should always mail them your bid-follow up letter. These office managers all had got one <u>before</u> I got the account.

Office number one was a doctor's office. The office manager showed me around the office and walked through it with me. Any medical type of office would already have a service in place to remove the red colored bags which are a biohazard.

<u>This is not part of the cleaning service.</u> This was a small doctor's office, and they only wanted it cleaned once a week. After the walkthrough, we sat down at her desk, and she wanted to know how much it would cost.

Bid # 1

Speaking with Mrs. Garrity, the manager at a small medical office

Sam: Mrs. Garrity, I would like for you to look at this first page of my service agreement. You see the 12 items listed there?

That is specifically what our office cleaning service always does as part of our routine cleaning. It is all spelled out right there. We do a thorough cleaning, not an easy cleaning.
Is there anything that you wanted us to do that is not listed herein these 12 items?

Mrs. Garrity: Well, let me look at this and make sure I understand exactly what you are going to do.

Sam: Yes, please do.

Mrs. Garrity: Alright, everything looks good. I would like it if you could water the plants when you are here. We have people here, our staff, that waters the plants, but it seems that everyone does it when they feel like it, and sometimes the plants get over watered or sometimes not enough, and they don't do well. If we knew that you did it once a week when you are here on a regular basis, then no one else would need to do it or think about it, and the plants would do better. Is that alright with you? Could you do that for us each week?

Sam: Yes, we can do it. You are talking about the nice-looking plants I saw in the lobby?

Mrs. Garrity: Yes, there is a bucket in the closet next to the kitchen. You can use that. Please be sure that you don't over water them.

Sam: Let me write it down. Water the plants in the lobby – don't over water them.

Sam: What was it about the previous cleaning service that was a problem, Mrs. Garrity?

Mrs. Garrity: Well, the cleaning service that we had did not do a good job. Here's one thing that really was a problem. They would come in and clean the kitchen, but we noticed that the sink was always a mess.

Sam: You are not talking about doing the dishes?

Mrs. Garrity: No, the staff here washes up after themselves. Everyone does their own dishes. I mean the counter and the sink. It just didn't look clean. Like they didn't wipe off the counter and wipe out the sink. It always looked dirty, and when we came in - in the morning, sometimes it looked the same as the day before, and it looked like it needed a good wiping off and wiping out in the sink.

Sam: I understand. We always give special attention to stainless steel sinks. We use a commercial product that shines them up very well, and it looks great. Is there anything else.

Mrs. Garrity: Sometimes, I left them a note pointing out about the countertops and sink, and the next day it was cleaned, and then the following week it would be dirty again, and I didn't feel like I had to constantly leave a note when it should have been done right the first time.

Sam: I understand. It can be difficult to find a good cleaning service. We do a thorough job.

Anyway, this type of office, and one of this size, that gets cleaned once a week has a price range that it could be cleaned for. Let me put these prices in here right now.(NOTE:(this is made on the price range chart, <u>not</u> on your service agreement) Here you go, look at this, please. It shows the range of prices from low to high. $85 to $125 dollars per individual cleaning. Is this price range in your budget for cleaning?

Mrs. Garrity: Yes, but I should tell you to be fair, that we are taking bids from other cleaning companies.

Sam: I understand, but does this seem reasonable to you Mrs. Garrity?

Mrs. Garrity: It does to me. Considering this is a medical office and everything has to be very sanitary. Yes, that would be in our price range.

Sam: That's good. That's where the bids should be no matter what cleaning service is doing it. Are you only looking for the lowest price bid?

Mrs. Garrity: Not at all. We don't want to hire the cheapest service.

Sam: That's good. We do more than most cleaning services. Would you like the cleaning service to be responsible for changing the burned-out ceiling lights?

Mrs. Garrity: That would be great if you could do that too. They don't burn out that often, but when they do it is so difficult to get up there and change them, so I would appreciate it very much if you would do that.

Anyway, $85 to $125 is fair for something like this. But how much are we actually talking about? That is a difference - $85 to $125.

Sam: Well, to include changing the lights and doing a thorough job of cleaning it should be $125 for once a week. I'll go ahead and fill out my service agreement for you based on that price right now.

Mrs. Garrity: Well, the other bids are not that high.

Sam: I understand, but is $125 dollars per cleaning too high? That's with the lights and watering the plants. That's $541.67 dollars a month.

($125 times 52 weeks =$6500,divided by 12 months = $541.67)

Will you give us the business for that price Mrs. Garrity?

Mrs. Garrity: Possibly so, the decision hasn't been made yet.

Sam: Well, here is the second page of my service agreement with the monthly price on it. ($541.67) Let me put a paper clip on these and leave it with you now. When do you think I might hear from you about getting started?

Mrs. Garrity: It will be next week.

Sam: Alright then, thank you for your time. It was nice meeting you.

NOTE: Get their business card with their address on it and mail your bid follow-up letter to them right away.

Bid # 2

Speaking with Louis - The manager of an accounting office.

The second office was an accounting office that required cleaning 3 nights a week. When I arrived at the office, the office manager showed me around with a walkthrough.

After the walkthrough, we sat down at his desk and immediately he took the lead and began telling me what a nice office it was ... they had very high standards, and he wanted to keep it that way. They already had a cleaning service but were not happy with them.

Sam: Thank you for letting me submit my service agreement. I appreciate it. Now, this is based on service to be provided 3 times a week. Monday, Wednesday, and Friday, is that correct?

Louis: Yes, that's right, but I don't want cleaning people in here before 5:30, because sometimes there are still people working.

Sam: Yes, I understand, but is it alright to start at 5:30? *Louis*: Yes,

but not before that time.

Sam: Well, here is the first page of my service agreement... it spells out exactly what our service consists of. The 12 items you see there are what we do when we are here. We don't just empty trash cans; we do a thorough cleaning for you. Is there anything that you would want our cleaning service to do in addition to what's listed there on the first page of my service agreement?

Louis: No, it is a general cleaning that we need done. This looks good.

Sam: What is it about the cleaning service you have now that you are not happy with?

Louis: Well, I know that they have different cleaning people in here all the time and they overlook things like forgetting to empty trash cans. Quite often we come in, and I notice that there are no paper towels in the restrooms. Sometimes there is not enough toilet paper in the stalls. I have left them notes about leaving extra rolls, but it still keeps happening.

Sam: I understand that, but my help has been with me for a long time now, and I pay them very well to do this type of work. We give special attention to the restrooms. Paper products are fully stocked in there before we leave, and we don't leave ring stains in the toilets. We also use a special stainless-steel cleaner where it is needed. We are a very professional cleaning service, and we do a thorough job.

I should tell you too that I would really like to have this account and I will personally be here on the job with my help.

Louis: You're going to be here, that's good to know! I think that is important, but we are taking other bids.

Sam: I understand. Are you only interested in the lowest price bid?

Louis: No. we're not going with the lowest price bid. We want a good cleaning service here.

Sam: There is a price range that an office this size can be cleaned for. Take a look at this price range chart I filled out for you. It can be done anywhere from $118. to $180. dollars for each cleaning. Does this seem reasonable to you?

Louis: I'm not really sure. We're taking other bids.

Sam: I understand but is this price range in your budget for cleaning?

Louis: Yes, it is.

Sam. Was the cleaning service you have changing the burned-out ceiling lights for you?

Louis. No... We were doing that ourselves.

Sam: I understand. To pay a maintenance service to change lights can really add up. We can include that for you in our service.

Louis: That would be good because I appreciate it when a person pays attention to details.

Sam. I'll write that down on my second page here. I understand you're taking other bids, Louis but I need to price it right, and I'd like your feedback on that price. Does $180 a cleaning seem fair to you? I'd like your personal opinion on a price within that range.

Louis: I think it's a little high.

Sam: O.K. well, I can lower it to $140, but I hope we get the account from you, Louis. You understand, I'm going to be here on the job and we are going to change the burned-out lights?

Louis: Yes, I understand that.

Sam: Is the $140 reasonable to you?

Louis: I think it is.

Sam: Will I have a good chance at getting this account even with other bids?

Louis: I think you do Sam, but I will still have to get back to you.

Sam: When might I expect to hear from you about starting?

Louis: It will be near the end of this month, that we go with a new cleaning service.

Sam: Great, well I look forward to hearing from you about it. I'd really like to take care of the office for you. Remember we do pay our cleaning help well, and we do a thorough job for you.

Louis: Alright then, I'll let you know.

Sam: OK. Louis, thank you, it was nice meeting you. *Louis:* You

too Sam

NOTE: get their business card with their address on it and mail your bid follow-up letter to them right away.

Bid # 3 - Speaking with Karen

The property manager of an office building with tenants

This third office was actually an office building with different types of businesses as tenants. The property manager of this office building was on site and employing a private cleaning service to take care of the entire office building 5 times a week.

When I arrived at the office, the property manager asked me to walk through the building by myself and then come back to her office to talk about it. After I walked through the building and looked at the individual units and the restrooms, I then sat down at her desk in her office, and she wanted to discuss the price.

As this was a large building amounting to over $1000. dollars a month I used the monthly dollar amount on my price range chart instead of an amount for an individual cleaning.

Sam: Thank you for letting me submit my service agreement to you, Karen. I appreciate it. Cleaning Service is to be provided 5 times a week in this building. Is that correct?

Karen: Yes, but we only need a complete cleaning done twice a week here.

Sam: A complete cleaning or full cleaning would include vacuuming and dusting 2 times a week here?

Karen: Yes, and once a week, I'd like the brass railing in the lobby to be cleaned.

Sam: We can do that, do you provide the brass cleaner for that?

Karen: I would do that.

Sam: That's good. Well, Karen, I'd like for you take a look at this. It's the first page of my service agreement. You see the 12 items listed there? That's what our routine cleaning consists of. Is there anything you would like us to do that is not listed on that page?

Karen: Well, is this is a full cleaning?

Sam: Yes, it is.

Karen: We only need that done twice a week here.

Sam: Yes, I understand, I'll write that down, and the brass railing gets cleaned once a week. That's not on the list, I'll write that down here and what about the elevator?

Karen: That needs to be kept clean.

Sam: Yes, we will keep it clean for you. I'll write that down here too. We would have one-price for the full-cleanings and one-price for the light-cleanings, but I'm sure that on a building this size, it's the monthly amount that is of most interest to you. I'd like you to take a look at this page.

(I handed her the price range chart)

It's a price range chart that I use. An office building this size can be cleaned anywhere from $2000. to $3000. dollars a month for 5 times a week. Is this in your budget for cleaning?

Karen: That's a big difference in the price.

Sam: Yes, it is, but it won't cost that much because you only need a full cleaning done twice a week and a light cleaning done 3 times a week.

Karen: What gets done on the light cleaning?

Sam: When the light cleaning is done, we empty all trash in the building, stock the restrooms and clean them.

Sam: May I ask you, Karen, how much have you been paying each month for the cleaning service that you have now?

Karen: Well, I don't like to give out that information and I should tell you that we have gotten 2 other bids.

Sam: I understand that but are the other bids over $2000 dollars a month?

Karen: Yes, they both are.

Sam: Do they include changing the burned-out ceiling lights for you?

Karen: No one has offered to do that. We have been doing it ourselves, and nobody likes doing it.

Sam: Well, on a building this size Karen, we are willing to include that service for no additional charge. Do you have a ladder here?

Karen: Yes, we do. It's downstairs in the closet.

Sam: Great, because I would need a tall ladder in this building and where do you keep the lights?

Karen: We keep them in that same closet with the ladder.

Sam: Well Karen, all things considered, we would like to take care of the building for you. The price should be $2400. a month and that includes changing the lights, cleaning the elevator, brass railing once a week and two full cleanings each week. Does this seem reasonable to you Karen?

Karen: Yes, but the decision has not been made yet. *Sam:* I understand but when will that be?

Karen: Near the end of this month.

Sam: Alright, well I look forward to hearing from you about it. It was nice meeting you.

NOTE TO READER
The original price I had in mind for estimating this account was $2000. a month. I did not tell her that, but after my conversation with this individual and using my own judgment, I decided to make it $2400. a month. So that is what I wrote down on my service agreement.

Reminder: Always get their business card with their address on it. After you submit your bid, mail your bid follow-up letter to them right away.

Writing Paychecks

The mechanics of writing out a paycheck for an employee is not really complicated at all. You can do it yourself with the guidelines that follow. You should understand, however, that, if or when you have around 6 or more employees working for you, then it can become a time-consuming chore so at that time you may want to pay someone else to do it for you.

There are many so-called, "payroll services" out there that specialize in doing that very thing for businesses like yours. They can be found in your local phone book.

In each state, the IRS has a booklet called the "Federal Withholding Income Tax Booklet" or more commonly referred to as "**Circular E**."

They are free for the asking, and you can get a copy of "Circular E and any other forms you may want or need from your local IRS office.

Circular E will also point out to you the necessary Federal and FICA deductions you need to take out from an employee's paycheck.

Any employee that you hire first needs to fill out a form for you called the "**W4**"form. On this form, they will be writing down the number of dependents (deductions) they are choosing to declare, and this will also influence the amount of money that gets deducted from their paycheck.

If your employee is getting paid an hourly wage, then you just add up their total hours on payday to arrive at the amount of money they have earned.

>Now...take that gross amount of the check and multiply it by .062 to determine the amount of money to be taken out for their **social security** deduction.

>Again...take that gross amount of the check and multiply it by .0145 to determine the amount of money to be taken out for their **Medicare** deduction.

>Each State has a different **State income tax** rate that is also required to be deducted from the employees check.

The State that you live in will normally mail you their withholding book for your use when you first register your business in your State. They will send you a form for taxes you might be subject to in your State.

For example corporate tax, income tax, employee's income tax, etc. Each State is different in regards to the state's income tax requirements.

For example, Michigan state income tax is 4%. Georgia state income tax is 8%, and California state income tax is 9%. Each State has a different income tax rate established for your employees, which is also influenced by the number of dependents they are choosing to declare on that "**W4**"form. Also, each State has a different tax rate for someone who is married compared to someone who is single.

The deductions above must be taken out from the gross amount of the check and then you <u>the employer, must match</u> the FICA and the Medicare amounts on behalf of the employee to be sent in with their total deductions.

"FICA" stands for, "Federal Insurance Contribution Act" and this is the social security deduction. After the deductions are taken out from the gross amount of their paycheck, the amount of the check that they actually receive is the "net amount."

Within 3 business days of writing out a payroll check, you need to then make a payroll tax deposit of all these deductions with a so-called, "Federal Depository."

Your local bank is usually the one who collects these tax deposits that you make on behalf of the Federal Government.

Hire Employees or Subcontract?

An employee is considered to be any person who normally works for you for either an hourly wage or a salary, but you take deductions out of their paycheck, and you control when they start work and when they stop work.

A subcontractor is considered to be any person who enters into a subcontract agreement with you and assumes some or all of the obligations and responsibilities of the primary contractor, who would be you, and your service business. They start and stop working on their own time and schedule, and are not working under your direct control.

The IRS is really somewhat vague on this subject, and there are many service business owners who employ both employees and subcontractors. The following information will help you decide which arrangement is best for you.

When it comes to service business owners, the IRS does not have a specific law regarding subcontractors. They do, however, raise the following 3 issues:

1. Under whose supervision is the person working?

2. Whose time are they working on?

3. Who has most of the control?

If the answer is "you ," then that person is an employee or yours. If the answer is "them," then they are a subcontractor of yours.

I have usually hired workers to be employees of mine and paid them an hourly wage. At times, I have also used the regular labor of a subcontractor to take on the full responsibility of providing service to a particular account of mine. Many service businesses only use subcontractors.

It depends a lot on which arrangement you are most comfortable with. When you are just getting your business off the ground, you most likely would have one person helping you do the work, and that person usually would be an employee.

This is not a requirement but a common situation in which case you would be responsible for the deductions taken out of their paycheck.

If you choose to hire subcontractors for your business, than a typical situation for paying them is to give them anywhere from 40% to 50% of what your customer pays you each month. You would then pay your subcontractor a fixed sum of money in the form of a check.

They would then be responsible for making any and all deductions out of the income they earn from you.

A subcontractor is typically responsible for having their own equipment, supplies, and insurance.

It is interesting to note that with hourly paid employees doing all of the work for you, it is common to see your labor costs running around 40% to 50% from the income that your business generates.

In comparison, you can expect 40% to 50% of what an account pays you, to be given to a subcontractor who takes on the total responsibility of the account on your behalf.

The customer pays you, and then you pay the subcontractor a fixed sum of money from the total monthly income of the particular account or accounts that your subcontractor is servicing for you.

It takes the same amount of effort to find a good employee as it does to find a good subcontractor.

On (the next page) is a sample subcontractor form that you can use:

Subcontractor Service Agreement

YOUR COMPANY NAME HERE

This agreement would be between you (the contractor)

and the subcontractor.

SUBCONTRACTORS NAME HERE

The contractor agrees to pay the subcontractor, for the service described,
The amount of $ dollars per month for providing service to
the following locations described below:

Job location:

Description of service to be performed by the subcontractor:Note: the subcontractor agrees to furnish and show proof of any and all equipment, supplies, labor, supervision, vehicle, insurance and anything necessary to do the work described in this agreement on behalf of the contractor and is acting and working independently on their own as a subcontractor. The subcontractor understands and agrees that they are responsible for paying their own taxes and the contractor is not responsible for any accidents of any kind which may occur during the work being performed by the subcontractor or their employees.

This agreement is dated:_____ .

Signed by the contractor: **YOUR COMPANY NAME HERE** Signed by the

subcontractor: **SUBCONTRACTORS NAME HERE**

Organize and Expand Your Prospect List

There is a very simple yet effective method of organizing customer prospects and leads that I have always used and it can very easily be done with index cards and an index card box.

If you are familiar with using the computer, you may prefer to do the same thing on your computer, or you can purchase special software at any office supply store to do this too. It's up to you how, you want to do it, but the main thing is to do it.

Here is what I am talking about. When you are making efforts to obtain a new customer for your service business, you may be doing any one of the following: personal visits, phone calls, letters, or postcards. Whatever it may be, a typical situation which commonly comes up is that the decision maker falls into one of several different categories or situations, depending on their circumstances.

The idea is this: you just use one index card for each potential customer and keep notes about them on that card. In your computer or in your index card box or software program, you have tabs with the name of each month of the year on them. Depending on what month you are in when you make contact with a potential customer is where you would initially have their card,

This is best explained by example:

Let's say you walk into a particular office and ask to speak with the office manager and they tell you that they already have a service. Should you leave it at that and walk out the door? No, never do that. Always make an extra effort to keep the conversation going with the objective of submitting your bid or service agreement to them.

Ask them, if they are on a contract with their current service and if so, when is the contract up? They may tell you that it is up in 4 months from now. When might they be interested in speaking with you again?

Do they have plans to move or open up a new office in town? Are they happy with the quality of work getting done by the service they have now?

Instead of being too quick to accept no for an answer, at least get some contact information, and write down a few notes along with the date of your initial contact, and the decision maker's name.

It was mentioned earlier but bears repeating, you should always ask if you may submit a competitive bid for them to keep on file.

So, what you would do is, write down your notes about this particular account and move that index card to a future point in time. Say 3 months down the road. Look at your cards every day, and when 3 months comes around, you will know to contact that decision maker regarding submitting your bid because their contract is almost up.

Always be moving index cards in front of others, to the future month in which you know for a fact that you can contact that individual decision maker again. This is somewhat of a leapfrog effect with the index cards, in which your index card filing system will result in a bid generator for you. It is really simple, but it works very well.

Keeping your own notes about a particular future customer on an index card or in your computer or software program will allow you to organize and expand your list of potential customers dramatically. This is a very simple and effective way to stay on top of opportunities that may otherwise be overlooked or forgotten.

You will find that your potential leads of customers will always be growing because you are making the most of every contact that you make. You start your list or so-called "customer cards" with one card, then two and on and on.

Just start looking at the notes that you have placed in the correct future contact month for the year, and by doing so, you will quickly find that you have a bid to submit almost every single week.

The results of this simple filing system and notes to yourself about the contacts you make are invaluable and are sure to keep you busy... growing your business.

How to Keep Your Customers Loyal to You Regardless of the Competition

Many service business owners go through so much to get a customer only to have them for a brief period of time before losing them to a different service business competitor. You won't be one of them because here is exactly how to keep them once you get them.

On the service agreement in the "Instant Office Cleaning Kit" that I have previously put together, (you should get it) you'll notice that at the bottom area of the service agreement there is not any kind of a statement implying that either the customer or the service business owner is locked into an agreement for any length of time.

This is fine when you are just starting out because, you really need to get started and get your first customer, and not having a so-called, binding contract takes some of the pressure off of the decision maker before hiring you and your service business. When they are first ready to actually sign your service agreement, it is up to you to decide if you want to include the sentence below which would turn your service agreement into a contract.

If you don't add the following sentence to your service agreement when it is first signed, then it is a good idea to add it after the first 12 months have gone by:

"This is a 12-month binding contract and can only be canceled by either party with just cause and a 30-day written notice; otherwise, renewal of this service agreement will take effect after each 12-month period of time."

This will discourage any thought of changing services on the part of the decision maker. There is no substitute for doing a good job, building trust and providing good service to your customer. That is what will really keep them loyal to you, no matter what.

Only by having these service agreements turned into contracts would it enable you to easily offer your business for sale at any time before the 12-month contract is up. If you ever decide that you would like to sell your service business in the future, then having your contracts in place would allow you to do this.

This does not mean that your price can never go up. It probably will go up in time. After you have been providing your service for 12 months you have developed somewhat of a relationship with your client, and they either are happy with you and your service, or they are not.

After 12 months of providing service to a customer, they are very receptive to a reasonable price increase. It is acceptable for any service business to increase their price after 12 months to keep pace with inflation and simply because after 12 months have gone by, you deserve a raise.

You can point this out to them verbally after 12 months and quite often have their total cooperation, or you can simply mail them a brief letter informing them of the new price increase that will take effect on such and such a date. If you mail them this notice after 12 months regarding your price increase, here is the wording that always sounds good:

ABC SERVICE COMPANY
                To whom it may concern: Date:

Effective on (such and such a date) we will have a small price increase in the service provided to all of our customers. This reflects our increase in labor costs, supplies, insurance, etc. and helps us to stay in business. The new price per month will be $$$. We appreciate your business and your cooperation. Thank you.

If you point this out in the service agreement that you initially give them, you may discourage them from hiring you and encourage them to get other bids. You don't want to do that, so just bring it up after 12 months have gone by.

It is normal to increase your price by an overall percentage, such as 3% to 5% a year. No reasonable manager or decision maker would disagree with that. Especially after they are familiar with you and the quality of the service that you provide.

Note: The first 12 months goes into effect once you actually start the job.

I have had many customers for many years, mainly because of the working relationship that develops over time. You can, and you should develop and encourage that yourself with every customer you get.

You do this by simply checking in with them, at least 4 times a year. Go in person and touch base with them.

Ask them if everything is fine? Would they like to see improvement in any area of the service that you are providing? If so, what is it? This is all it takes to ensure a lifelong, loyal, happy customer. The majority of services just don't do it much, or they make the mistake of neglecting to do it at all.

Always keep in touch and involved with your customers either, by phone, in person or by leaving notes on their desk. The message you are getting across to them by doing those things is that you care about keeping them as a customer and it does matter to you that they remain pleased with your service. You just need to communicate with them on a regular basis.

Correct any small problems before they turn into big problems, and in most cases, your customer will never want to hire anyone else. In fact, they will basically tell any other service that approaches them to forget about it because they are very happy with the service they have and they have become somewhat of a devoted and loyal customer.

You already know that the appearance of your service agreement by itself will really help to separate you from any other cleaning company.

(On the next page) is a cover sheet to be used when you submit your bid. You can use it with the 2-page service agreement that is contained in this Kit.

Adding the cover letter will make a difference in the appearance of your bid. This is just one more thing that will give you an edge when bidding and gain you favor from any decision maker!

Cover Sheet for Your Bid

(Put your company name here)
Licensed and Insured

Professional Cleaning Contractor

Using the 3 words "Professional Cleaning Contractor" on your cover sheet will help you establish credibility with any decision maker and further distinguish you from competitors. No matter which cleaning service a decision maker chooses, they favor a professional service and having these words on a cover sheet will remind them that you are a professional.

It would also be a good idea to list on the bottom of the cover sheet any affiliation with trade associations or if you are a member of the Better Business Bureau (BBB).

You don't need any such affiliation right now, but later on, if you do join any type of trade organization, BBB or even your local Chamber of Commerce, the bottom area of the cover sheet would be a perfect spot for pointing that out with either a logo or the words, "Member of...

I should remind you again that your bid (now 3 pages) should always be put into a large envelope (without folding any papers) available at any office supply store. This will add to the overall presentation of your bid and again imply quality.

When your bid looks professional, it is a logical conclusion that your cleaning service must be professional too. You can find these folders for about one dollar or less, and it is worth it to submit your bid in this manner.

Answers to the most Frequently Asked Questions?

1.Question: What form of legal entity should my business be?

Answer: This is an important decision to make when you are just starting your service business. You don't want to have to change the name of your business in the future for any reason. So, you need to get it right, to begin with. The legal entity that you decide to use for your service business will most likely be what is called a "sole proprietorship." After several years, I became an "S Corporation" in the state I live in.

The only effect this had on the name of my business was that Inc. (which is short for incorporated) was added onto the end of my business name.

The laws in each state tend to be slightly different. I suggest you call a few local accountants in your area. You will find they will be very willing to answer your legal entity questions for you over the phone for free. They hope you will become a client of theirs in the future and you very well may.

Also, talk with your local banker as they open a new business checking accounts for people every day and are familiar with these laws in your area and can point you in the right direction.

An accountant will ask you a few questions that will help you to determine what is best for you. Questions such as: Do you have or want a partner? If you die, do you want the business to continue? Do you want your personal finances to be separate and protected from your business?

2. **Question: How much should I pay my help?**

Answer: Well at this time, I start off my help at $10 dollars per hour. After 30 days have gone by and if they are doing a good job and doing the work well, then I increase their hourly pay by 50 cents per hour. They know this up front and also that they are on a 30 day so-called, probation period.

You may find that due to the area you live in that hourly wages are somewhat higher. If this is the case, then you would need to make a small adjustment in your square foot estimating prices. Not in regards to how long it will take to clean, because that will not change, but in regards to the higher cost of your labor. 2 people can perform the routine cleaning of 2200 sq. ft. of office area in approximately 30 minutes.

You can always keep that in mind and use that as a guide to double check your final price. As a rule of thumb, it is normal to double your labor costs. So, as hourly wages go up, make an adjustment on your estimating chart to compensate for this increase in labor costs.

2. **Question: I live in a large city. I think I should raise my prices because of where I live. How high can I go and not price myself out of the competition?**

Answer: If any adjustment needs to be made in your price because of living in a large city, the adjustment will hinge on the difference in the worker's hourly wages. Here is what I suggest: If you think that a good, fair

wage to pay your workers is $15 dollars an hour instead of $10 dollars an hour... then add $10 dollars to the total price for each individual cleaning.

4. Question: How do I hire good help?

Answer: Bad help is very easy to find, just hire anyone and you'll wish you had not. Many people need to make extra income, but many people do not make the best cleaning help for your service business or any type of service business. You ideally are looking for a person in particular circumstances and with particular qualities.

Ideally, here is what you should look for:

1. Someone who has a good work ethic.
2. Someone who has experience in commercial cleaning
3. Someone who has been at their present place of employment for at least one year.

An exception to this is someone who is perhaps a homemaker who for whatever reason does not need to be working at a full-time job but has plenty of time in their day to work at... a part-time job in the evening hours.

Note: it is a good idea to put the words, "experience preferred" in any help wanted ad that you place in your local newspaper.

5. Question: Should I increase or decrease the charge for my individual service visits, if the customer wants the work done once a week instead of five times a week?

Answer: Yes. Let me give you an example here. Suppose you are talking to someone who, for whatever reason, only wants to pay for your service, once a month. This would mean that when you come by once a month to do your cleaning or whatever service you perform, there will be an unusual accumulation of time-consuming work to do.

The work very well may need to be done once a week but thinking that they are going to save lots of money, they only want the cleaning service to come in once a month.

The fact is, <u>the less often</u> the service is performed, the more you should make an adjustment upward in the individual price per cleaning. The <u>more often</u> the service is performed, the more you could make an adjustment downward in the individual price per cleaning. The frequency of your service does influence the price of your service.

In other words, if I determined that I was going to charge $80 dollars for my work to be done once a week but the customer only wanted it done once a month, then I would double this price to $160 dollars, and it would be worth it.

The most common situation that arises is someone either wants your service done one, two, three, or five times a week. Normally, I would only consider a break in price for my cleaning service if it was a large account and the frequency of cleaning was going to be done five times a week.

6. **Question: I often hear the decision maker tell me that they already have a cleaning service. What should I say to them?**

Answer: What you should say is this: "I would like to submit a competitive bid for you to keep on file. Things do change", especially if they have a bad service. To submit your bid should always be your objective, <u>then</u> mail your bid follow-up letter, and <u>then</u> call them on the phone a few days later.

Don't be too quick to give up just because someone already has a cleaning service. Whenever possible be sure to wipe off the top edge of any pictures or paintings on their wall to show them just what kind of a cleaning service they are actually paying for.

Usually, you will wipe off tons of dust on your fingers which quite often knocks them off their feet and... opens up the door for you and your bid.

6. **Question: I am trying to figure out a price to charge for cleaning a fitness center. It is not really an office at all, but they want me to give them a price for cleaning. Should I still go by the square foot estimating chart that is in your original "Instant Office Cleaning Kit"?**

Answer: There are many different types of businesses that employ a private cleaning service but are not really similar in any way to a typical office. You should always charge more for them, than the usual price for this type of account. Write down on your service agreement the particulars of what they want cleaned that are not already listed on your service agreement and charge an additional sum of money for the work. Increase

your individual price per cleaning before determining the total monthly bill. An adjustment in price is always justified for factoring in more time-consuming work, the level of difficulty, more than 2 restrooms, etc.

8. **Question: Do I need to go into the office and see it before giving the decision maker the price?**

Answer: Yes, you should always look at the job or the office before you actually come up with a price for doing the work. You could give them the price when you are there looking at the job or if you are more comfortable with having more time to think about the price, then you can simply tell them that you will fill it out and bring it back to them. If you do bring it back, do it as soon as possible.

8. **Question: Can you go into more detail for me regarding the pricing of large buildings in comparison to pricing the small offices?**

Answer: I have always recommended that anyone just starting out in their own cleaning service go after the smaller offices rather than the large office buildings.

The square foot estimating chart in the popular "Instant Office Cleaning Kit" goes up to 10,000 square feet. The prices that are next to the square foot figures reflect the price for an individual cleaning.

The large office buildings are quite often cleaned by the large cleaning companies. If you are going to bid on them and try to get one of these big office buildings than you need to price them like the larger companies are pricing them.

Generally speaking, the large buildings that are all cleaned 5 times a week are priced at 9 or 10 cents a square foot, multiplied times, the total square footage of the building to come up with the total monthly price.

Again, this 9 or10 cents times the total square footage of the building, will not give you the price per individual cleaning but it will give you a price for the entire month based on providing cleaning service 5 times a week.

Most individual jobs, both residential and commercial, have 2 restrooms in them. Most jobs require that you do the routine cleaning described in the service agreement that you should already have.

However, there are some jobs that will want or need you to do extra work which is not part of the normal routine cleaning.

Whatever so-called, "extra work" may need to be done should always cost more. How much more? This will have to be a judgment call on your part based on how long it will take one or two people to do the work. For example, I have never seen an extra restroom that isn't worth adding at least $10 dollars more to each individual cleaning that gets done.

When you are looking at extra things to be done, and you are not sure how long it will take to do them, then you should keep in mind that 2 people can do the routine cleaning of 2200 square feet of office space in about 30 minutes. This same amount of square footage would take one person about one hour to do.

Knowing this will help you to determine how long it takes to get the routine cleaning done, but it will not tell you how long it will take to do extra oddball jobs, not a part of the normal routine cleaning. Your service is paid by the job, not by the hour. However, extra work should be priced based on the time and difficulty involved in doing it.

As a rule of thumb, you should always charge the customer double your hourly labor costs (what you pay your help), and you keep the increase in price for extra work or extra jobs that need to be done. Sometimes there are extra tasks that are not part of the routine cleaning that the customer will ask you to do.

For example:

If a customer says to you that, next time you are here providing your service, they would like to have their 2 ceiling fans wiped off, or a ceiling light bulb changed then what that would mean to you is this:

You or your helper is going to have to stop doing whatever routine service they are in the middle of doing, climb up a ladder and do the work. Then put the ladder back where it belongs. This may only take 20 minutes to do, but I would round that up to 30 minutes.

So, if your help is costing you $10 dollars an hour, then it just cost you $15 dollars or $5 dollars more in labor costs. Because of the $5 dollars more in labor costs, you should now increase your bill to the customer by $10 dollars.

In other words, if the job normally costs the customer $90 dollars, then it will now cost them $100 dollars. If you are not sure how long it will take to do the extra work, then tell your customer that you will have to do those extra things (anything not listed on your service agreement) for an initial price of such and such, but after the initial first-time work is done, then you will give them a permanent price for doing it on a regular basis. After you have done it one time, you will know exactly how long it takes to do it.

10. Question: Is it a good idea to charge more for the initial, first cleaning and if so, how much more?

Answer: Yes, it is a very good idea to do that. The majority of the time, a new customer in the cleaning business has changed services because the previous service was not doing a good job.

Chances are...you are walking into a big mess that will take 2 or 3 normal routine cleanings to bring it back up to par, so to speak. It is best to charge more for an initial cleaning because, the first time that you do the cleaning, it will take you much longer to do.

If the normal price per cleaning was determined to be $80 dollars per cleaning, then you could go as high as double that price to $160 dollars for the initial first-time cleaning.

First time cleaning always requires that the inside perimeter of the office or home needs to be vacuumed using a hose or portable vacuum along the baseboards, before vacuuming the open areas with an upright vacuum cleaner.

Also, toilets and sinks usually require twice as much work on the first cleaning. After that first cleaning is done, you can begin the regular routine cleaning which will maintain the appearance of the home or office on a regular basis.

Make the Income from Your Office Cleaning Business Last a Lifetime

I have seen many business owners of both residential and commercial services remain in a rut that they just never get out of. The problem is they start off their service business with good intentions, and they work hard, but they are always doing the physical work themselves.

Being a business owner is a great thing, and when you first start your cleaning service business, it is normal to be involved in the work yourself. Especially when your business is small, and you only have just one or two people helping you.

You may want to keep it small, but as your expectations grow, you will want to keep growing your business. When you are just getting started, you want to keep your costs down and be prepared for expenses down the road. Things like a new piece of equipment or a new part-time helper. This is how it all starts off.

Just remember that you should initially be the one who sets the standards for your help ...of how the work should be done and how long it should take to do it.

Owners who always stay involved in doing the physical work of their business find themselves participating to the point where they are not happy with the business they own but only because they quite often become burnt out from doing so much of the labor themselves.

It does not have to be that way at all. You can position yourself and your service business to where it will actually run itself quite efficiently without you being there all of the time. In fact, you can spend your time as you please.

In the long run, wouldn't you prefer to own a service business in which other people are doing all of the work for you? Most people would prefer that, but as I said, they get stuck in a situation that just seems to never end, and they don't know how to change it.

I'm going to explain to you how to change it, and the sooner you start working on this plan, the better.

In a nutshell, you want to hire people to do the work for you, so you have the time you need to work on getting more customers and better managing your workers and your business.

That challenge can be difficult but you need to do the more important things of growing your service business, and you need the time and energy to do it ...

So, you should have a plan and a purpose to get your business where you want it to be. Always look at the bigger picture.

You always start off with one account, but you should make efforts to obtain at least 3 or 4 new customers each year.

Take the time now and make whatever changes you need to make in order to phase yourself out of the physical work. This may mean a brief and temporary cut in pay, but it is worth it, I assure you. It is a temporary trade-off of your time to be used in a much more productive manner, and the long-term results will be well worth it.

To transition yourself from doing the physical work to a management position, you will need to hire someone to replace yourself.

This will mean a temporary drop in your income. Only now, you will have the time to get another new customer.

Each new customer you get will increase your profits and offset any loss of income you may have experienced, from personally doing the work, as you begin to manage it instead. You can, and you will still own, run and manage your business, but you will put on a different hat, so to speak.

NOTE: It is normal to expect that when using employees or subcontractors, your labor costs will always run you around 40% to 50%.

The only way to ever get into this management position is to take the steps that you need, in order to get yourself where you want to be. Also, as you begin to get more customers, your income will continue to increase, even though you are now managing the work and not participating in it.

You must break away... so that you can expand your customer base. This is the only way to get yourself into an absentee owner management position which will enable your business to grow and still make you a profit.

Even if you only grow it to a certain point and then choose to keep it that size, it is only by positioning yourself as the owner / manager of the business that your business can continue to provide you with an income every month. By doing this, your cleaning service business can and will provide you with an income that will go on and on...even if you do retire and go fishing every day.

When you are ready to make this transition and replace yourself, you will want it to be with someone who is responsible, dependable and hardworking. Someone like you. This person will be your first so-called "key person" who will fill your shoes on the jobs. This key person will be a working supervisor. They will participate in the service getting done, and they will be in charge on your behalf and in your absence.

This key person will normally have, keys, a shirt with your company name on it to wear. (even if they are a subcontractor), equipment, a cell phone and the responsibility for the quality of service provided to your customers. The responsibility that you used to handle will now be their responsibility.

You may want to start out managing your service right away, and that can be done, but I recommend that you wait until you have obtained around 5 customers for your service and 3 part-time people working for you.

This is the point when you can and should make the transition from working to managing because this is when the management plan would ideally start.

Every service business begins with just one customer. Your first and only customer would not need or require any management at all unless it is a very large account that needs your service often. An exception to this will be if you put a subcontractor to work for you right away.

When you are first getting started, and you get your first customer, you really need to be on the job yourself (which is a great selling point), and you do not have enough work or hours to be assigned to someone else yet anyway.

When using the labor of either subcontractors or employees, you will find the transition into management to be a smooth one, if you do it after you already have several customers who are paying for your service.

There are many books that have been written on the subject of business management and even college degrees in business management. All of these typically center on the subjects of accounting, record keeping, and advanced math and various paperwork tasks or chores.

I have even seen them turn the subject of inventory control into rocket science. As a service business owner, the only thing you need to know about inventory is this: "When supplies are low, you need to get more of them.

"Of course you should have some idea of when you should order or purchase more supplies based on how quickly you are using them, but you will learn that very quickly, as you gain experience and begin the work on each job. Anyway, all of these topics (above) are chores that you as a service business owner can delegate to someone else as need be.

To manage a growing service business in the real world, you don't need to be a jack of all trades and a master of none. You just need to <u>get more customers,</u> get a <u>good price for your service, hire good help</u> and primarily, <u>make the transition</u> from doing the labor to managing the labor that gets done.

I have seen several successful owners of their own cleaning service who after many years in the business, we're ready to get out of it and did so by giving notice to their customers and simply walking away from what was a valuable and steady source of income. It didn't have to be that way at all.

It brings to mind an old saying "is it better to keep the cow, sell the cow or just get rid of it? If you keep the cow, you can keep milking it and always continue to get milk from it. So why ever get rid of it?

Acquire good people to work for you and help you run your business. People you trust who will do a good job and get paid well to run your business without you. This way you can keep the cash cow as long as you want and continue to make an income from your service business as long as you want to. As long as you keep it.

Focus your efforts on these areas alone, and there will be absolutely no limit to how large your business and your income can grow.

In all walks of life, there are people who are good at what they do, and some are bad at what they do. Even if they are a college graduate in business management, that does not mean they will be a good business manager of a cleaning service. Especially if they have never actually been involved with one.

Listen, you can be very good at what you do including the management of your own service business without any special education or college, and you don't ever need any outside manager. You are the only manager you will most likely ever want or need for your cleaning business. You just need to find yourself good people to help you get the work done and who do a good job for you.

As soon as you have a few customers and a small crew of workers, (usually just 2 or 3 people), you can begin this new role of manager, and you manage a small growing service business the same way you manage a large service business. So, when you do begin that management transition, you should plan on making the most of it. Grow your business big and fast. Grow it to be small or grow it to be large. It's up to you.

With the simple bid generating method explained in the section: "organizing and expanding your customer list," you will become very proficient at submitting bids on a regular and consistent basis because you will quickly develop many leads and appointments to go on.

Your new role as the owner / manager of your business now becomes one with 2 main responsibilities. **Getting customers** and **managing your labor**.

With this information and a little effort on your part, you can literally take total control over your service business and also grow it as large as you want it to be. Either way, take control of it now because otherwise, as more and more time goes by, it can take control of you.

A strategic game plan for growing your business is to understand the different tasks or responsibilities required to keep it organized and efficient. There are 3 areas to focus on:

1. **Sales**, includes bidding, getting leads and customers.

2. **Labor**, includes hiring , training, and supervisors.

3. **Management** should ultimately be where most of your time is devoted to. This can include things such as billing, account receivables, payroll, and taxes.

You get the idea. You can always add more items to the areas above such as computer work and adjust them as need be to your own liking. To delegate the tasks of growing your business will keep it organized and enable you to grow your cleaning business much faster too.

Overlooked Tax Deductions

It is very important that you understand both the IRS definition and position when it comes to tax deductions for your service business.

Here it is:

<u>Any</u> ordinary or necessary business expense associated with your service business...*AND*...<u>anything</u> related to the production of your service business income can be used as a tax deduction including this e-book purchase.

Many things in a service business are overlooked that could be used as a tax deduction and should be used. Many of the things that you could use as a tax deduction may seem small or insignificant to you, but if they come under the definition (above), then you should use them as a deduction.

When you put all of the various deductions together, you will find them to be not only substantial, but they will add up to the point where you will save money every year.

Here are two main things you should consider using as a tax deduction:

The IRS-Actual Method

Your vehicle: Whatever car, truck or van you may be using for your service business requires lots of gas every week, and this gas expense can be used as a tax deduction.

Every penny associated with the expense of your vehicle in the operation of your service business such as, what you spend on gas, oil, maintenance and repairs can and should be used as a deduction 100% of the time.

Get and keep your receipts for everything. This method of using 100% of your vehicle expenses 100% of the time is referred to as the... "Actual Method."

The IRS-Standard Method

Regarding the deductions of your vehicle under the so-called... "standard method," you would need to keep track of your mileage by keeping a record of it and take the mileage and multiply it times the standard mileage rate. For example, that rate is currently... "forty and one-half cents" per mile. This standard mileage rate that you can use, usually changes each year as the price of gas goes up.

Each year the IRS comes out with the new or current mileage rate that you would use. The IRS usually comes out with this figure in October, November or December for the coming year.

It is a good idea to speak with a tax professional about your service business and what is new with the tax laws even if you handle it all yourself. You could also ask the IRS by calling them anytime on their toll-free phone number at 1- 800-829-1040

NOTE: An important factor you need to understand about either the "Actual Method" or the "Standard Method" is this:

If you operate your service business out of your home, then you can Include the driving expenses of your vehicle from the moment you leave home for work as you drive from account to account... to the moment you get home from work.

If your office is not located in your home, then you can only use the mileage that takes place as you drive from one job to another job.

The main thing to keep in mind regarding what qualifies as a tax deduction is an expense that could be related to running your service business, and I do mean anything! You know best what your expenses are.

Use them all and keep those receipts! They add up substantially and with a little record keeping on your part the savings to you from any, and all tax deductions you can come up with will save you money.

The Home Office Deduction

The home-based office deduction is a good one, and you can take advantage of it if the office area in your home really is an office and not used for any other purpose.

It could be a small room, a porch, or any area you like but your home office area must be used exclusively for business purposes. Technically speaking, no personal items like a bed or even a TV set can be in that area unless there is a business purpose for it.

What you do is this: Measure the square footage of the area or the room in your home that you use as your office and use that figure as a percentage of the total square feet of your home. You only need to take these measurements one time.

Then you can use that percentage that your office space consists of and deduct that percentage from your mortgage payment or your rent. You can also deduct that percentage from your electric bill.

Also, you should assign a percentage of business use to your home phone bill and use that as a deduction also.

Many people, who have a cell phone, use that primarily for personal use and deduct their entire home phone bill as a business deduction for their service business.

Here is an example: You use one room in your home for business. Your home has 4 rooms, all about equal in size. Your office is 25% of the total area of your home. Your business percentage is 25%

Also, remember that regardless of which type of legal entity you set up for yourself, such as a sole proprietorship or a corporation you should always keep your business checking account and expenses, separate from your personal checking account and your personal expenses.

You may also want to get a credit card for your business expenses which will help you to keep more accurate records for tax purposes.

Use this information as a guide and discuss your tax deductions with a tax professional in your area.

Little Known Resources You Can Use for Your Cleaning Business

Below are the best business-oriented websites that you can use to help you in operating your cleaning business. They are very beneficial websites to access, use and continue to learn from. Check them out.

#1 www.iprint.com

Sooner or later you're going to need some business cards. Save time running around and go to this website instead. To order business cards, you choose a card template and start filling in text. 46

You can pick the font size you like, graphics you may want, paper quality and preview your work before ordering your business cards. Need help with iprint? Email them at Customer_service@iprint.com

#2 www.ssa.gov

This is the official website of the U.S. Social Security Administration. You can search for a variety of subjects from taxes to social security including benefits for the self-employed. Need help with ssa.gov? Call them toll-free at 1-800-772-1213

#3 www.entrepreneur.com/howto

This website is really a wealth of articles and information to look at. There are many updated articles of interest to self-employed people from health insurance, to getting started and also incorporating your business

#4 www.nase.org

For an affordable membership fee, you can join The National Association for the Self-Employed. They offer many benefits for self-employed people such as a towing service, health care discounts and much more. One unique benefit they offer is a pre-employment background screening service. Call them toll-free at 1-800-232-6273

#5 www.sba.gov

This is the official website of the United States Small Business Administration. There are many free articles and topics of interest for the self-employed such as business start-up basics, marketing information, tax forms and much more. They have a huge library of information online for any business owner. Call toll-free 1-800-827-5722

Always ask what it was about the previous service that was not getting done properly in the decision maker's opinion. It is logical and reasonable for most people to be willing to pay more for a better job to be done. After all, if they were happy with the cleaning service they had, they would not be talking with you now.

Also, keep in mind that you are not speaking with the potential customer to make new friends with them. You need to remain somewhat distant and businesslike when you are discussing your service business. After your business meeting is finished, you can begin to develop a good business relationship with your customer, and you should, because there is just no substitute for the trust you will earn from them as time goes by.

Whatever you decide to do, remember, "in all labor there is profit"

Proverbs 14:23

CONCLUSION

Get copies of the various sales letters and documents made up with your own company name on them. Also get some envelopes and a few business cards ready. Use your computer and keep the information updated or use a small file box with index cards for each contact that you make and keep the information updated. For example:

Mailed introduction letter 7/25

Follow-up phone call 8/15
Mailed reminder letter 9/15

Mailed postcard message 10/15

Note: A bid was submitted for service 3 nights / weekly, for a monthly amount of $1480.on10/29

Include the address, phone number, and name of a specific person. Send mailings to their attention.

One at a time, build up as many contacts as you can. First, call the office and speak with the office manager or visit the office in person and get their business card, then mail out the introduction letter.

If you don't know the name of the decision maker, just ask, and they will tell you. If they want to know why you want that person's name, tell them it is because you are going to send them a letter about your business and you want to send it to that person's attention.

Get the correct spelling of their name too. You'll only need to do this one-time for your notes.

Whatever methods you use, I have outlined for you a direct advertising program at its best. It costs pennies, compared to any other form of advertising and it is much more effective because you are going directly to the decision makers.

If you work the methods explained in the Kit, the methods will work for you. Things change. People quit. Cleaning services that start doing a bad job get replaced. Opportunities open up. Keep trying to get a customer, and you will get one. Put out the bids as often as possible, mail your bid follow up the letter and before you know it, you'll have all the business you can handle.

Don't depend on any one way of getting customers. Work on different things and always keep in mind that your goal is to submit a bid, mail the bid follow-up letter and then call them again.

You'll notice on the introduction letter that it begins with the sentence, "Thank you for the time and hospitality given to me as we discussed"

If you have actually spoken with a decision maker in person or over the phone, then you would mail them the introduction letter as is. If you have not yet spoken with the decision maker and you still want to mail a letter, then simply remove the first sentence of the introduction letter. Prepare two different introduction letters that are both ready to use. One letter with that first sentence on it and one intro. letter without the first sentence on it.

Do some direct phone calls, and do some walking in, right off the street. Mix it up a little. Do what you can as you have time to do so but be sure to do something to promote your business every week.

I have seen many times when someone is just starting out in this business that when they keep trying to make new contacts and submitting bids, that something takes place. Not always right away but it does happen. What happens is they suddenly have one breakthrough after another. One new account comes through for them and then another and another.

Some bids that you submit may not contact you until 3 months later. They may realize that they should have gone with your service instead of the lower priced one that they did go with. You never know, so stick with it.

Regarding direct phone calls to office managers, be sure to make these phone calls and use the phone script as a guide.

Be sure to specifically say:

"I would like to submit a competitive bid for you to keep on file because things change."

Phone calls to offices have proven to be effective and are exactly what the franchise cleaning companies do to get new leads and new accounts.

You can do it too or have someone help you do it. Also, anytime you are driving around and notice a new office or building under construction in your area, or you see a vacant office, act as a private investigator and write down whatever phone number is posted and track down who it is that is going to be moving in there as a tenant. Contact them with an intro. letter and/or a phone call, because they are prime prospects.

Stay on top of the best prospects with phone calls and reminders every 30 days. Check back with them (specifically the decision maker) and communicate with that specific person. Your objective is to submit a bid to them (in person) then mail your bid follow-up letter, then call them.

Now of course if an office has a good cleaning service, they should keep them, but most do not have a good cleaning service, and they should make a change for this reason.

If they want references from you, you can simply use a few personal references with names and phone numbers. Give that to them on paper. Yes, you need a break to get started, but someone will give you a break in this business if you remain persistent about getting accounts.

I don't think it is easy to start any business, but it is much easier to start an office cleaning business and much more affordable too. Your risk is practically non-existent. It is limited to your time and some postage stamps. In time, you will have your own following of customers who are loyal to you regardless of the competition.

When you are just getting started in this business, it means

that you can be on the job. This is of tremendous value, and it is a selling point. Just starting out is an advantage, not a disadvantage.

Offices are not going to be doing you a favor by giving you the account any more than you are doing them a favor by cleaning it, so, you don't need to beg for the account and come across as desperate. You do need to keep in touch and communicate with the decision maker in a professional manner.

This is how you will be in the right place at the right time.

Start your own top 10 list of names and addresses of businesses in your area that you know employ a private cleaning service from speaking with someone at the office or building. Be sure to include the individual's name (the decision maker) in the notes on your list.

It is fine to start with just 10 contacts and then grow your list from

there but always concentrate on your best top 10 and remain persistent.

Now, it becomes a numbers game. You can increase the numbers in your favor by growing your list, making more contacts and keeping in touch with them.

What you should do with that list is phone calls, letters, reminders, / phone calls, letters, and reminders. All with the purpose and objective of submitting your bid to them and then always mail the bid follow-up letter after a bid is submitted.

Sometimes I have gotten a new account simply because of that bid-follow-up letter. It shows how professional you are and decision makers are impressed with it.

Quite often I came to find out that I was the only one who even mailed them such a letter. It is a professional touch, and that will work in your favor.

Work on more than one way of getting customers such as phone calls and walking in off the street in person. If you do walk in cold, don't leave their office without getting their business card and the name of the decision maker.

Don't mail out large quantities of letters at one time. You want to call the offices after mailing a letter so only mail out small quantities at one time.

You could fax or mail the introduction letter and then follow up with a phone call. Either way would be fine, but I favor a traditional letter because it makes it more personal.

When you do add a new contact to your list, be sure to include the decision makers name. Mail a letter to the attention of the

decision maker (on the outside of the envelope in the lower left corner

put (**ATT**: then (the decision makers name). You can simply hand write it on the outside of the envelope. By doing this, your letter

looks personal. It's sure to get past the receptionist and into the hands of the right person.

When you do call the office back, ask to speak to that specific person by name. Whenever you go in person to visit an office or with an appointment to see the manager, wipe off the top of any picture frame or painting on the wall with or without their permission. Just do it (in front of them) and show them ALL THE DUST that comes off the top of it. Dust

build up is also very common on the tops of partitions (stall dividers) in the restrooms. Show it to them because all this dust build up will speak for itself.

Why would any sane person want to continue to pay for a cleaning service that is NOT doing a good job for them? They don't, but they also

don't want to be a pushover either so don't push them to do anything except to accept a free estimate from you. You just want to give them something for free right now. You want to get your (filled out) bid into their hands. Don't leave a blank bid with anyone.

You do need to be in the right place at the right time, and this is done by keeping in touch with the people on your list. I have seen many times where new accounts come through as a direct result of being persistent.

The second they realize they want or need a new cleaning service, they will be calling you with the utmost respect.

I wish you success and would like to remind you that you can always contact me if you would like a second opinion on the price of a bid, or you have any questions about the Kit or the cleaning business. Be persistent about getting started and getting accounts.

Remember, persistence prevails if all else fails. Especially in the office cleaning business. You can always make a new contact or check back with old ones and update your notes. There is always something you can do to promote your business. Offices are all around you so get busy. The potential for your success in this business is unlimited.

The square foot estimating chart in the Instant Office Cleaning Kit makes it easy to price offices that are under 10,000 sq ft.

When you are to estimate a building that is OVER 10,000 sq. ft., It is done this way.

There is an average of 22 cleaning days a month on an account that is cleaned 5 times a week.

Multiply your total sq. ft by .10. That will give you a monthly amount based on cleaning 5 times a week.

Now divide that monthly amount by 22 to determine the individual price per cleaning.

For each restroom over 2 restrooms, add $5 dollars onto the individual price per cleaning. Then multiply your new price per cleaning by 22 to get the monthly amount based on cleaning 5 times a week.

On accounts that want your service 5 times a week, you should always offer them 2 different scenarios on your bid or 2 different prices for their consideration.

One price for a full cleaning done 5 times a week. The other price for a light cleaning/full cleaning schedule. That would be where a full cleaning is done 2 times a week, and a light cleaning is done 3 times a week.

A light cleaning would only include getting all the trash and checking the restrooms and restocking them. Nothing else. On your light cleaning nights, you can cut the price per cleaning in half.

I do think it is best to go after smaller accounts. Accounts that do not require service 5 times a week. That's because I have found that an account that is done 2 or 3 times a week is more profitable than an account that is done 5 times a week.

Even though a 5 night a week account may pay $3000 a month or more and a smaller account may pay $1200 a month.

I prefer the smaller accounts. I'm sure you would too.

A smaller account is easier to do. Typically requires less labor cost and the individual price per cleaning is actually more profitable than that of a large building that is done 5 nights a week.

Join Affiliate Program and Earn Additional Income

Help promote the website, http://www.CleanUpTheProfits.com and sell The "**Instant Office Cleaning Kit**" and The "**Instant House Cleaning Kit**" on the internet to other interested people. Both Kits come with great customer support after the sale. The affiliate program and the commissions are all tracked and handled by a very reputable transaction company called "Clickbank."

I will split the profits with you 60/40. You will get 60 percent of the profits from each sale that you help to promote. This is a generous commission plan and a good affiliate program. For more information on this affiliate program, go online to:

http://www.cleanuptheprofits.com/affiliate.htm

>>> 4 Bonus Reports <<<

In addition to the routine cleaning, the following information will give you an overview of the most profitable services that offices typically pay for. At some point, you may want to include one or more of these services to go along with your office cleaning business.

While in the process of operating your own office cleaning service, you will most likely come into contact with people who already own and operate one of the following 4 services and it would be in your best interest to at least be familiar with them. Network with these other business owners for the purpose of promoting your own business.

Note: If you are interested in starting your own House Cleaning Business, be sure to look at http://www.CleanUpTheProfits.com/homekit

> 4 Bonus Reports <

The 4 Most Profitable Add-On Services

That All Offices Must Have and Will Pay For

4 Special Bonus Reports Pages

In addition to the routine cleaning, the following information will give you an overview of the most profitable services that offices typically pay for. At some point, you may want to include one or more of these services to go along with your office cleaning business.

While in the process of operating your own office cleaning service, you will most likely come into contact with people who already own and operate one of the following 4 services and it would be in your best interest to at least be familiar with them. Network with these other business owners for the purpose of promoting your own business.

Note: If you are interested in starting your own House Cleaning Business, be sure to look at http://www.CleanUpTheProfits.com/homekit

---

Bonus Report #1

Carpet Cleaning

The carpet cleaning industry is a billion dollar a year business. Many homes and office buildings built since 1960 have wall to wall carpeting in them. Most every office has a commercial type of flat pile carpeting installed in it. Wall to wall carpeting is a big investment, and people want to make it last as long as possible. They do so by paying for a carpet cleaning service to clean their carpet at least once a year.

Restaurants are also considered a commercial cleaning job like an office, but restaurants generally have their carpet cleaned more often than offices do. Residential carpet cleaning includes houses, apartments, condominiums and "rental properties."

There is a constant need for carpet cleaning to be done and it is growing all the time. You could operate your own carpet cleaning service on a small scale for extra income or make a growing business out of it and bring in at least $50,000 dollars a year or more.

You can get lots of residential carpet cleaning jobs from real estate property managers who manage rental properties, because every time a renter moves out, the carpet gets cleaned as does the entire unit. Contact these property managers and offer your service to them. You only need one property manager to start using your service, and you'll get a substantial amount of business from them.

Residential jobs will primarily come directly from the homeowners themselves. Homeowners typically vacuum their carpet on a regular basis, but they usually pay to have it cleaned once or twice a year.

The "do it yourself" carpet cleaning people who rent a machine when they need it, are no cause for alarm as they will not affect your success in the carpet cleaning business. Most people are just too busy to handle all the "do it yourself" chores that need to be done around their home.

People also procrastinate and put off doing any chore that requires special equipment like cleaning the carpet. You will find that most people will be very willing to pay you to show up with the equipment and do this work for them.

It doesn't take any special skill or experience to operate a carpet cleaning machine. Anyone can do it. It's a service business you can start one day and have money coming in within a week. You can start this business in your own neighborhood, and begin making a profit almost immediately.

You can get started in this business and earn $250 per day or more with no upfront investment by renting what you need when you need it.

The most important thing to remember about this business or any type of service business is to always continue your marketing efforts. All service businesses succeed, primarily due to the marketing efforts put into promoting them. Your success in the carpet cleaning business will depend on the effort you put into getting customers.

You have to sell your service to potential customers. Eventually, getting carpet cleaning jobs lined up on a regular basis will become easier for you. You'll have all the business you can handle if you stay with it and get through the start-up stage. It will be to your benefit to learn all that you can about promoting your carpet cleaning service.

The most common method of cleaning carpets is referred to as "steam cleaning." It got that name from the steam that rises up from the carpet as the hot water is being used. The carpet is not actually being cleaned with steam.

It is getting cleaned by injecting hot water into the carpet and extracting it using a wand and suction power. There are truck mounted units that do this and portable units. All you really need to get started in this business is a good portable unit. Before you ever buy or rent any carpet cleaning equipment, you need customers.

Your prime customers are every business, office, restaurant, and home in your area with carpet on the floor. The work ahead of you is in reaching these prospects. Your objective is to convince them to hire you and your carpet cleaning service. Then get them to set up a time for you to do the work.

The least expensive method of reaching these people is by way of neighborhood handouts or flyers delivered in person door to door. These flyers are advertisements that should be announcing a "Carpet Cleaning Special."

Your flyer will be like having your own advertising billboard. You should be able to get 2 flyers off of one standard size sheet of paper. Have a printer cut them in half for you with their paper cutting machine after running the copies for you. That way, if you have the printer run off 500 sheets and cut them in half, you will get 1000 flyers out of it.

The objective of this type of flyer is to invite the recipients of it, to call you for an appointment to show up and clean their carpet. Look at the ads for carpet cleaning companies in your local newspapers and in the yellow pages of your telephone book. Also, look for any similar flyers you can find.

Your flyer for homeowners should advertise a special, for example:

**YOUR LIVING ROOM CARPET, DEEP- CLEANED
FOR JUST $49 DOLLARS!
WE GET THE GROUND IN DIRT, SPOTS AND
UNPLEASANT ODORS OUT FOR YOU.
WE CAN DO IT ALL FOR YOU TOMORROW!!!
GIVE US A CALL TODAY. SET UP A CARPET CLEANING
APPOINTMENT WITH US NOW.**

**WE'LL HAVE YOUR CARPET SUPER CLEAN, READY
FOR COMPANY, IN NO TIME AT ALL!**

PH.123-4567
"SPRING FRESH CARPET CLEANING SERVICE"

Prices that are charged on commercial jobs such as offices and restaurants range anywhere from 20 cents to 30 cents a square foot. In this case, you would simply measure the total amount of carpet and charge a price per square foot. Being able to advertise "All work fully insured" will add a lot to your business image.

Using a pen or pencil, write out your own flyer on a blank sheet of paper, and take it to a printer to be typeset and have copies made. You may already know how to do this yourself on your own computer. If not, a local printer will help you with the design and layout of your flyer.

You just have to tell them what you want it to say. While your flyers are being prepared, you should be making plans to have them delivered. These flyers can be put out by anyone of the following:

- do it yourself
- with help from a friend or relative

- college or high school students

Whatever arrangements you make to distribute your flyers, be sure that you have someone available to answer your phone and set up appointments for you if you can. The next best thing would be for you to have an answering service or an answering machine and be sure to call people back, as soon as possible! You could also have potential customers call you on your cell phone number.

The special offer advertised on your flyer should only take you about one hour in the customer's home. Depending on the travel distance between appointments, you can schedule one job to be done, every 2 hours.

Offering a special deal is the key to getting your foot in the door of residential jobs and flyers are a great way to promote this special. A big tip you should know about to do a great job is to use some kind of carpet spot cleaner before you use the carpet cleaning machine.

There are some excellent carpet spot cleaners on the market today. They are either in the form of a liquid, foam or powder.

Whatever spot cleaner you choose to use, it's a good idea to pour it into one of your own spray bottles to use in the customer's home or office before cleaning the carpet.

Regarding residential work, always try to line up several carpet cleaning jobs to be done on the same day. This will become easier to do as your business gets off the ground. Every time that you do a residential job, you should write down the customer's name, address and phone number on an index card along with the date that you did the work, and exactly what was done for how much money, or you could keep this information on your computer.

These people should then be called every 6 months about setting up their next carpet cleaning appointment.

Try to line up a few appointments for the same day or two consecutive days. Then get over to your local janitorial supply store. They are advertised in the yellow pages of your local phone book. Some of them have a much larger selection of products and services than others so you may want to talk to them on the phone before driving all over town.

What you would be looking for from them is to rent a portable carpet cleaning machine. Many "rent everything" type of stores and some supermarkets will rent a portable type of carpet cleaner, but you will find that the type of portable machine available from the janitorial supply store is much more powerful than the portable machines available elsewhere.

Some of the larger janitorial supply stores will allow you to rent to own, or extend credit to you and let you make payments on a portable (commercial quality) carpet cleaning machine. When you are just starting out, you can simply rent a machine for about $40 dollars for 24 hours. Make sure that you understand how to operate it from the business that is renting it to you before you drive off with it.

Load it into your car, van or pickup and go to your first appointment. This method is profitable, and it works. This is exactly how to get started with no money invested in purchasing equipment.

Usually, a carpet cleaning service takes you directly into the homes of your customers. Therefore, beginning with your very first job, you should always project a professional image. A pullover shirt with a collar and your company name on it is a good way to do this.

You could also buy yourself a uniform from almost any department store. Either way, if you are simply using a pullover shirt as a uniform, you should have your company name put on it. How you dress and handle yourself in a customer's home has a direct influence on the success of your business. When you do hire someone else to help you with the work, be sure to have that person dress accordingly too.

Go out of your way to be polite and friendly to each customer. Concentrate on getting the work done so you can move on to your next job. When you are providing the cleaning service to a particular office, you are there every week, and you have an ongoing working relationship with the office manager.

Just talk with the office manager and tell them that you now offer that service also and you would like to do it for them when they are ready to have it done. At this point, it is very easy to be the one who gets the next carpet cleaning job from them unless you prefer that another company provides them with that service.

You should make it a point to always speak with the neighbors who are directly on each side of your customer's home or office. As long as you are already doing work in the area, they might like to go ahead and have you clean their carpet or their office for them too.

Always leave a business card with everyone. If you are in a customer's home cleaning their living room carpet, the customer may ask you about the cost to do the other rooms in their home. Give them an estimate, for example, $39 dollars for each additional room or so much per square foot and do the work right then if possible.

A typical carpet cleaning job will end up involving more than just one room with an average cost to the customer of anywhere from $80 to $250 dollars. Your cost for materials on each job will only cost you about 4 dollars for the small amount of detergent you will be adding to the water. Anyway, with just 4 appointments per day, five days a week, your income before expenses would fast be approaching $1000 dollars per week. It adds up fast!

Many people who set up their own carpet cleaning service bring in $50 thousand dollars or more their first year. You get out of it what you put into it. Be creative and always put efforts into getting new customers. You have read about how to get started with practically no out of pocket investment. However, you should either purchase or lease your own carpet cleaning equipment as soon as you can.

Usually, the service you would be providing is referred to as: "the deep-down steam cleaning" of carpeting in homes or offices. Always try to use the best carpet cleaning machine that's available to you. Eventually, you'll want to lease or buy your own equipment.

Your business will grow and prosper as a result of your always doing a good job. When you are just starting out and learning to use and work with the equipment, it may take you a few minutes longer than you expected to do an extra good job.

Developing a group of satisfied customers is the key to your becoming successful in this business. Satisfied customers will call you back for more, and they will help to spread the word about your service for you.

There are many similarities in the office cleaning service compared to the 4 services described in these 4 bonus reports. Many of the same things would need to be done regarding any type of service business.

For example, regarding any type of a "home based business", as long as you don't put up a billboard on your front lawn for all the world to see that you are operating a business from out of your home, you won't have any problem working from your kitchen table or a spare room.

Also, sooner or later, you'll have to get yourself a business license. The sooner you do this, the better you'll feel about your business and the more confidence you'll have about what you're doing. If you wanted to, you could have one business license and one company name that would encompass several different types of services all under one roof.

If you decide to do a full-time business out of carpet cleaning, then check on the cost of running a quarter page ad in the yellow pages of your local telephone directory when you can afford to do so. You'd be surprised at the number of calls you can get from these ads in response to a carpet cleaning service.

However, just starting out, you should run a small display ad in your local weekly paper. Sort of a scaled-down version of the advertising special that you advertise on your flyer.

Traditional radio or television advertising does not work well for this kind of service when you compare the costs involved to the number of phone calls you get from it. I would suggest, however, that you check into doing some local cable television spots. The cost to advertise on cable TV is very reasonable.

If you ever want your carpet cleaning service to grow really big, then as soon as you can, hire other people to do the work for you. The best way to do this is to hire people to work as a cleaning team of 1 or 2 people. Then your only job would be to get customers lined up, see that your employees are doing a good job and keep everything running smoothly.

Starting from scratch, this is a low-investment, low-overhead type of business for anyone who wants to make it on their own. A carpet cleaning business of your own is one of the easiest service businesses to start and operate. It's a service business that can grow very fast and bring in the additional income you desire.

Remember, that almost every customer you work for will have you come back on some kind of regular basis, even if it's only once a year. You would be building up a repeat customer base, and it adds up fast! Understand, that marketing your service business is an ongoing continual process. It never ends.

You should put some effort into marketing your service every week. Decide on your own plan of marketing and stick with it! The profit potential for an owner of this type of service is excellent!

Bonus Report # 2

Pressure Cleaning

If you enjoy working outdoors and don't mind getting a little wet, then you can clean up the profits in your own pressure cleaning service. There are very few businesses which allow you to put down as little as $500 to $1000 dollars and start making money right away.

You could also find yourself a good used pressure cleaning machine for even less. There are incomes reported in this business of $180,000 dollars a year and more. A one-person operation with one machine can expect to bring in at least 50 to 60 thousand dollars a year.

Just working this business on a part-time basis for extra income can earn you $30 to $40 dollars per hour or more. Basically, what you need to know is this: The P.S.I. rating on a pressure cleaning machine is what determines its power. P.S.I. stands for "pounds per square inch."

Pressure cleaning machines with less than 1200 P.S.I. are usually not strong enough to do the job effectively. Pressure cleaning machines that have more than 2500 P.S.I. could cause damage to the surface being cleaned. You should use a pressure cleaning machine that is capable of at least 1500 P.S.I. to 2500 P.S.I. You should also be using a machine that pumps out 4 and1/2 to 5 and1/2 gallons of water per minute.

The design and the size of the nozzle on the end of the wand are also important as they affect the width of the spray pattern. A 15-inch spray pattern is good; however, you should always hold the nozzle only 10 to 12 inches away from the surface being cleaned at approximately a 45-degree angle. This is the correct way in which pressure cleaning should be done.

The most common recommended nozzle size for pressure cleaning a house or the outside of a small office building is a 15 or 25-degree nozzle.
This will give you the best results and allow you to do a very controlled cleaning.

You may be cleaning the outside of a house, office building, overhanging eaves, a driveway or storefront of some kind. Whatever you may be pressure cleaning, the cleaning detergent you use will depend on the job and how dirty the surface is to be cleaned. The surface may need to be pre-treated with a brush and a cleaning liquid first. Often, a clear water pressure cleaning will do the job just fine, without using any kind of detergent.

If there is a lot of oxidation or mildew on the surface to be cleaned, then you should use a general all-purpose cleaner, available where you rent or buy the pressure cleaning machine. The purpose of using chemicals is to emulsify surface dirt. If you use some type of chemical or detergent with your pressure cleaner, it can be applied to the surface being cleaned in one of 2 ways:

The first way would be to simply use a brush on a pole and dip the brush into your cleaning solution. Then apply to the surface before using the pressure cleaning machine.

The second way would be to use a small device called a downstream injector which simply attaches to your pressure cleaning machine with a coupling. This injector will enable you to apply a detergent at the same time that you are spraying water onto the surface.

A small hose would be used and simply go into a 5-gallon bucket of detergent. The other end of the hose would go into your injector. Clear water and detergent would then come out of the wand in one step.

Some pressure cleaning machines already have a downstream injector on them, and some don't. You can have one put onto a machine that doesn't already come with it, or you can just use a brush and pole to apply the detergent if need be.

Either way, you should dilute your detergent (according to directions) ahead of time in a 5-gallon bucket that would sit next to your pressure cleaning machine.

When you first start using a pressure cleaning machine, you'll be working with a large amount of water pressure. (about 1500 to 2500 P.S.I.) In comparison, the average household garden hose delivers only about 60 P.S.I. While a common garden hose can wash off loose dirt, it cannot remove ground in dirt, stains and pollution build up. High-pressure water used with a general-purpose detergent can clean practically any surface.

If you're going to be pressure cleaning an exterior wall or overhang that is beyond your reach, then you will want to use a telescoping spray wand to go along with your pressure cleaning machine. If you're using one of these extension wands, be prepared to hold on tight. When you pull the handle to start the flow of water, the wand will kick back about 3 feet. The more experience you get in using the pressure cleaner, the easier it will become for you to control the wand.

Learn all you can about the different types of chemicals, equipment, and surfaces to be cleaned from a supplier who specializes in manufacturing, selling and renting pressure cleaning machines. They can provide you with technical support and answer any questions you may have about the machine.

For example, a hot water pressure cleaning machine would be desirable if you're going to be pressure cleaning restaurant kitchens because there is so much grease everywhere. Cold water pressure cleaning would still get the job done in a greasy kitchen, but it would simply be more time-consuming.

When you're just starting out in this service, a cold-water pressure cleaning machine is all you need. They work great on almost any type of surface. Also, a hot water pressure cleaning machine costs about twice as much as a cold-water pressure cleaning machine. Anyway, after you have been in the business for a while, you may prefer to use a hot water machine.

If that's the case, you won't need to get a different machine as you could simply purchase a portable hot water generator which would turn your cold-water pressure cleaner into a hot water washer.

Keep in mind, that most customers don't know or care whether you are showing up with hot water or cold water. Most people in this business are using a "cold water" pressure cleaning machine. Anyway, the water does not actually come out cold. The temperature of the water increases just from having it pass through the machine. Powerful and portable pressure cleaning machines are available at most rental equipment stores and at the larger janitorial supply stores.

You can also rent the telescoping wand for upper story walls and hard to reach overhangs. As mentioned earlier, you should locate a specialized dealer of pressure cleaning machines to do business with as they will be more helpful to you whether you are renting or buying the machine.

If you start out by renting a pressure cleaner instead of buying one, first line up several jobs on the same day or on the same weekend. That way, it will be a very profitable weekend for you, even though you rented the pressure cleaning machine. Your customers don't know whether you rented it or not and they don't really care about that.

As long as you are renting the power washer that you need, the key to making it really pay for itself, is in lining up more than one job ahead of time, to be done on the same day that you rented the machine. Also, for an additional fee, you can offer to pressure clean more than one area for the homeowner or for the office building manager, such as sidewalks, driveways, steps, overhangs, entrance areas, exterior walls, roofs and even trash cans.

First, clarify exactly what's going to be cleaned for how much money, before starting the job. The price you charge to do a particular pressure cleaning job depends on you. When you are just starting out in this service, you should become familiar with the prices that competitors in your area are charging, and you should base your price on how long you think it's going to take you to do the job.

After you have done a few pressure cleaning jobs, you will have a very good idea of how long it is going to take you to do the next job that you get. For example, vinyl siding is the easiest and the least time-consuming surface to pressure clean, but wood siding is the most difficult and the most time-consuming surface to clean. Whatever the surface is that you are going to pressure clean, (wood, vinyl, brick, concrete or stucco), feeling confident about what to charge is simply a matter of experience.

In many cases, you can get the job even if your price is higher than a competitor's price. Just make sure that the customer understands what a complete job, he or she is going to get.

For example, point out to them beforehand that you will cover all outside light fixtures with plastic bags and duct tape. Also, that you will cover any electrical outlets on the exterior walls with some plastic or polyurethane film and duct tape.

You should also place a plastic drop cloth of some kind over any plants or shrubs around or underneath the overhang or exterior walls. Most people appreciate and value extra attention and detailed work. A fabulous selling point for getting most pressure cleaning jobs, (even at a higher price) is to clean the outside of the windows after the pressure cleaning is done. When the potential customer hears that you will include the cleaning of the outside windows, it makes the job a lot easier to get.

The next time you are driving around your area of town, start looking at the condition of houses, storefronts, overhangs and entrance areas of offices. The area where you live may be ripe for a new pressure cleaning service.

The outdoor elements all take their toll on various types of surfaces. The dirt build-up is very unattractive and can cause permanent stains and
damage to the surface. So simply look for jobs that obviously need to be pressure cleaned. Then, find the manager, the decision maker or the homeowner.

Whoever it is, give them a business card and tell them, " you would like to pressure clean their storefront, overhang or the entrance area for them. Whatever it is, mention that "it really needs to be done." Downplay the price by waiting for them to ask you how much it will cost. Quite often they will hire you on the spot to do the work and pay you right away.

Don't underestimate the power of this direct approach. When you look for things that really need to be pressure cleaned, you can find them. They are everywhere, and the chances are that the manager or the homeowner will agree with you. Quite often, they have just been putting it off and are glad you stopped by and pointed it out to them.

You could also try to get a commercial account which is done more often in comparison to a house which is usually done once a year. For example, gas stations are good commercial accounts. The outside bays where the gas pumps are located and the overhang above the pumps usually get pressure cleaned, once every 3 months and you can charge at least $300 dollars or more for this type of commercial account.

The alternative to getting customers by the direct approach is to pay for advertising. Advertise with a Yellow Page ad in the phone book for this type of service when you can afford it. When just starting out, advertise in daily or weekly newspapers in your local area. You can also talk with your local cable TV station about doing some 30 second still spots. Cable TV is very reasonably priced.

The best advertising is word of mouth, but that will slowly develop as you do more and more jobs. When a person sees one of your ads in the newspaper and calls you for a price to pressure clean their house or whatever, it is important that you present yourself in a business-like manner. Always point out to them that you need to stop by first and see the house or building in order to give them a price.

Pressure cleaning is also a great way to prepare the surface of a house or building for repainting, and it is normally done by professional painting companies before they start painting.

So simply give your business card out to each and every painting company in your area because they may already be too busy painting to do all the pressure cleaning jobs that they come into contact with.

A thorough pressure cleaning will remove dirt, moss, and mildew so that the new paint will adhere properly to the surface. Not only that, but many people find that they don't even have to paint at all after the pressure cleaning has been done.

You can actually save homeowners and
businesses, hundreds of dollars and prolong the life of their existing paint job. House washing is where the bulk of customers come from, but the following list of additional sources of income from a pressure cleaning service is sure to keep you busy.

- Houses
- Tile and asphalt shingle roofs
- Mobile homes

- Recreational vehicles (camper, RV's, airplanes)
- All types of flat concrete (patios, porches, sidewalks, driveways, garage floors and entrance areas of offices)
- Steps (concrete, wood or brick)
- All types of siding (aluminum, steel, vinyl or wood)
- Storefront entrance areas
- Overhangs and eaves
- Concrete and tile entrance areas of convenience stores
- Fleets of vans or trucks
- Gas stations
- Construction/farm equipment and mill machinery

TIPS FOR A SUCCESSFUL PRESSURE CLEANING JOB ARE:

Always wash the surface from the bottom up and then... rinse it, from the top down. Otherwise, the detergent and dirt will run down the wall and leave streaks or stains on the unwashed surface.

Always make sure that any of the glass windows are closed, and never spray directly on the windows because the water pressure can cause damage to them.

When pressure cleaning a garage floor or a driveway, you may find that it works best to first use a commercial degreaser (applied with a brush on a pole) to emulsify the grease and oil and then pressure clean the surface.

Be careful not to put your hands anywhere near the end of the wand when the pressure cleaner is operating as the extreme pressure can cause the water to penetrate the skin.

Always watch out for any overhead electrical power lines and keep the wand at least 10 feet away from them. If it is necessary, you can clean the area around the power line on an exterior wall by hand using a wooden brush.

All you would really need to start making money from this is a business license, some business cards, a pressure cleaning machine and the information contained in this report. Most people in the pressure cleaning business really enjoy making money outdoors and having the freedom of being their own boss. You can start cleaning up the profits too! The money is just waiting to be made.

Bonus Report #3

Window Cleaning

The window cleaning service is the easiest of all service businesses to start. In any city and town, on any day, you could walk down the street with the right know-how and tools and come home with cash in your pocket. More glass windows are being used today in the construction of homes and buildings than ever before.

Storefronts up and down any street are typically covered with large sheets of glass windows in the front of their business. Offices not only have glass windows on the outside of the building, but they normally have glass windows, glass doors and glass partitions on the inside of their office as well.

Glass windows are everywhere, and they need to be cleaned on a regular basis. All you need to be performing this service is the following:

- A large empty 5-gallon bucket
- A 17 and 1 half inch squeegee
- A window cleaning mop
- A razor scraper
- Towels and rags
- A small step ladder
- "Joy" dishwashing detergent
- "Parsons" lemon fresh ammonia

Understand that there is a difference in so-called window or glass cleaning solutions.

The one that you would use which is similar to "Windex" in a spray bottle with paper towels is the formula you can get for free in the upper left corner of my website located at www.CleanUpTheProfits.com
The window cleaning formula that you would use with a squeegee is different from the glass cleaning formula that you would use in a spray bottle. You could go to your local janitorial supply store, and they would be glad to sell you some kind of expensive, ready to use, window cleaning solution, but that is just not what you would need to be using.

All you need to do is this:

Take a large empty 5-gallon bucket (you can purchase one of these at a paint store or a home supply store) and fill it up with water.

Now take a bottle of "Joy "dishwashing detergent, turn it upside down and squeeze it into the water for just 2 seconds.

Next, take a bottle of "Parsons" lemon fresh ammonia and pour about 1/3 of the bottle into the bucket of water.

Now stir it up a few times with your squeegee. That's all there is to it. It works great and leaves the glass sparkling and clean. This is exactly what many professional window cleaners use, and it costs very little.

There is really only one well-known company that manufactures window cleaning equipment and their name is " Unger ." Their products are available at any janitorial supply store which you can find in your local telephone book.

Anyone can walk into this type of store and buy anything they want. You don't have to already be in business for yourself, so to speak. Go into one of these stores and ask for assistance. Have them show you the various window cleaning tools that they have so you can become familiar with them.

The window cleaning procedure is to simply dip the window cleaning mop into the bucket of window cleaning solution and then apply it to the window. Now, just use the squeegee to take it off and wipe the window sills with a towel or rag. Learning to use the squeegee properly and quickly is a matter of experience and practice.

The professional way of using it is done in a so-called "butterfly method" in which you simply start with the right corner of the squeegee in the upper left corner of the window and start moving the squeegee to the right side of the window in a vertical position.

Now, you lower the right corner of the squeegee as you lower the squeegee down the glass and move the whole thing vertically back to the left side of the window. Before you get back to the left side of the window, you start to lower the upper left corner of the squeegee and then move the whole thing in a vertical position back to the right side of the window. Just keep repeating this process until you get to the bottom of the window.

You may want to use a dry towel to wipe the water from the perimeter of the window and the sill. Anyway, that's the butterfly method, and it can only be learned well and done quickly by practicing it.

You could start out by simply moving the squeegee in straight lines from top to bottom and, overlapping each stroke by one or two inches. This will work too but the "butterfly method" is faster.

If you encounter any dirt or debris on a window that seems to be stuck to the glass, that is when you would use a razor scraper before or during the cleaning of the window. The main thing you need to know about a razor scraper that is used on glass is to never dry scrape with it.

In other words, always put some liquid on the glass, in the area where you are going to use the razor scraper. Always wet scrape or you could scratch the glass. You could apply some of your window cleaning solution or spray some of your glass cleaning solution on the area where you will be using the razor scraper first. Either one would work just fine with a razor scraper.

If you are going to be cleaning any small square shaped window panes, you can clean them by simply using your spray bottle solution and some paper towels instead of a squeegee.

This is generally an all-cash paying service business. Most customers pay you in cash on the spot as soon as you are done with the job.

NOTE: all of the services described in this bonus part of your kit are not part of the so-called, "routine office cleaning service." You are not expected to provide these "add-on services," but only to recommend someone for these jobs when need be.

Exchange business cards with other business owners and you will always have a company that you can recommend. Hopefully, they will return the favor by recommending your office cleaning service when the situation arises. This is networking. You can, and you should network with many different service business owners.

So exactly how much should you charge to clean windows? Well, I can tell you this. The prices of window cleaning services vary tremendously. Once you become fast at doing it, you should easily be able to earn yourself $30 to $40 dollars an hour or more for doing this type of service.

Just start out by getting a feel for doing the work and how long it takes you to do it. You become faster at doing it with experience. Charge a fair and reasonable price when just starting out and become familiar with what the other window cleaning services in your area are charging.

You can easily do this just by calling some of them on the phone and asking them questions. Questions like: Do you have a minimum charge? How much do you charge to clean the windows on the outside of a one-story house?

How much do you charge to clean storefront windows? For example, the front of a convenience store?

You could also be upfront and honest with store owners and managers of offices and tell them that you are just starting to clean windows and you are not sure exactly what to charge, so would they help you out by telling you what amount they paid to have them done the last time.

Some people will tell you and some will not. If it is an office that you are already cleaning, they will be happy to tell you, because you will have already established a good business working relationship with them.

The only window cleaning that you would most likely ever concern yourself with is what is referred to as "groundwork." Groundwork is any windows that you can reach and clean while you are standing on the ground. If the use of an extension pole, a short folding ladder or even a small step stool is necessary for you to reach windows that are higher off the ground than this would not be considered to be "groundwork."

Windows (on the outside only) that you can reach and clean from the ground could be charged at "so much per window, " and windows that are higher should cost twice as much per window.

You can approach the pricing of window cleaning jobs in one of two different ways. One is to charge "so much per window, " and the other would be to simply estimate how long it will take you to do the entire job. In other words, a price per window or a price per hour.

Only from starting to actually do this work will you get a feel for how long it will take you and how much you should charge. You could build an entire window cleaning business around "groundwork" jobs by themselves because there is so much of them all around.

Now that you are familiar with this window cleaning service, you can do any one of the following with this know how.

- You can start your own window cleaning service business.
- You can make extra money by providing this service to your own office cleaning accounts.
- You can have a professional window cleaner give you an estimate for a job to be done that you mark up the price on, and profit from it as a middleman for this service.
- You can simply network with other window cleaning service owners for the purpose of promoting your own office cleaning business. It's all up to you.

Bonus Report #4

Floor Care

If you get satisfaction out of seeing a job well done and appreciate the end result of your efforts than you will really enjoy operating your own **(V.C.T**.) floor care service. With such a low investment, huge profits to be made, a rent-free office in your own home and no experience needed, this is an ideal service business for any person wanting a highly lucrative service business of their own.

Keep reading, and you will learn how you can get started with no investment in equipment. All that's really needed is a business license and the information contained in this report. You can start this business and begin making big profits almost immediately.

This business is simply referred to by some people as "stripping and waxing." It is in fact, a professional floor care service performed on V.C.T. flooring. The letters "V.C.T." stand for "Vinyl Composition Tile."

This type of floor is normally identified by 12-inch squares of vinyl. This type of commercial floor covering is commonly found in the majority of all offices and commercial establishments. This V.C.T. flooring requires regular maintenance, not only to prolong the life of the vinyl floor but also to keep up a shiny new appearance.

Many offices have at least some area in their office, (such as the kitchen or hallways) where you can find this type of flooring. Many grocery stores, drug stores, and convenience stores employ a professional floor care service to work on their vinyl flooring every single night.

These types of commercial establishments have so many people walking through their store every day that the V.C.T. flooring they have, requires maintenance on a daily basis to maintain a high gloss appearance.

Commercial establishments other than grocery stores usually have their V.C.T. floors worked on either once every week, once every month or on a quarterly basis.

The types of commercial accounts that typically employ a floor care service are the commercial establishments that you should contact when starting out in this service business:

- Grocery stores
- Drug stores
- Convenience stores
- Medical and doctor's office treatment rooms
- Office cafeterias and lunch rooms
- Lobbies and hallways
- Hair salons and barber shops
- Car dealerships
- Department stores

PLUS...any of the many other places you can find in your area that has V.C.T. (Vinyl Composition Tile.)

Wherever there is V.C.T. flooring, there is a constant need for this lucrative service. You can do this service business on a small scale for extra income or make this service business grow and bring in $50,000 to $100,000 dollars a year or much more! The basic equipment needed to perform this floor care service consist of the following:

- Wet-dry vac
- Mop heads and handles
- Mop bucket and wringer
- Buffing machine

Also, depending on the customer and the frequency of the floor maintenance at a particular account, you will want to have access to the following:

- Wax (called "floor finish")
- Stripper solution
- Floor sealer
- A mild neutral floor cleaner for scrubbing.

There is a specific type of mop-head that you should use to apply the floor finish or wax. I recommend a mop which is a blend of rayon and cotton, preferably, rayon only. There is a so-called "finish mop-head" which is made entirely of rayon.

This type of mop-head will spread out the wax (floor finish) more smoothly and give you better-looking results. You simply place the mop on the floor and slowly pour about one cup, at a time, of wax onto the mop-head. Then you just start mopping the floor to apply the wax.

The names of the big 3 companies that manufacture floor machines are:

- Kent
- Advance
- Clarke

A "buffing machine" or sometimes referred to as a "floor scrubber" which is what it is mainly used for, is a floor machine which operates at a slow speed. That speed is around 175 R.P.M. The letters (R.P.M.) stand for... (revolutions per minute). You should only use this machine for stripping and/or for scrubbing the floor.

The other type of floor machine is called a polisher. This type of floor machine will have anywhere from 300 to 1000 or more R.P.M (revolutions per minute) and should be used for polishing only. You could use a buffing machine to polish a floor with but it would just be more time-consuming.

Large round pads that are made of a polyester blend go to the bottom of these machines, and the pads are held in place by brushes on the bottom of the machine. These pads are identified by color, depending on which job you are going to be doing.

A black colored pad, which is the more abrasive of all the pads, is used for stripping floors along with a commercial stripping solution.

A blue or brown colored pad is used when you are just going to be top scrubbing a floor with a mild commercial scrubbing solution and then recoating it with wax.

A white colored pad, which is the least abrasive pad is used for polishing floors, in which case you would simply use some floor finish in a spray bottle and spray a small amount on the area you are about to polish with the white pad.

Normally, an initial stripping, sealing, and waxing is done to a V.C.T. floor. After that has been done, the typical job would involve a weekly, monthly or quarterly maintenance schedule.

Generally speaking, you can charge anywhere from 20 to 30 cents a square foot for doing an initial job of stripping, sealing and waxing.

What you should take into consideration when pricing the job, is if you are required to move furniture and put it back when the wax dries. This should be understood beforehand. If the customer wants their furniture moved and put back after the floor is cleaned, then they should have this done before you arrive to do the work. If they do not already take care of this for you, then your price should reflect the additional work required on your part to be moving furniture for them.

Also, become familiar with the price per square foot other people in your area are charging. You can just call and ask them this on the phone, and you will have a good idea of what square foot prices are being charged for this kind of service.

THE PROCEDURE AND FREQUENCY

This initial type of job, consisting of 3 steps... (stripping, sealing and waxing) is normally done only once a year. Usually, it is not even done that often, but when it is done, the floor would be stripped, then a wet/dry vac would be used to get up excess liquid, then the floor would be mopped with clear water.

Two coats of floor sealer would then be applied to the floor and four coats of floor finish / wax. Use one mop-head for sealer and a different mop-head for the floor finish.

NOTE: mop-heads can be machine washed in a regular washing machine. but you do not need to put them into a dryer.

If your floor maintenance job is to be done on a once-a-week basis, then you would typically sweep or dust-mop the floor first, THEN, machine scrub it, THEN, high speed polish the floor and spray some wax on it as you go, (using a spray bottle with wax or floor finish in it).

On this type of once-a-week account, you would scrub (top scrub) the floor and put more floor finish on the floor (re-coat) with 2 to 3 coats, once every 3 months. If the customer's floor does not get too much traffic and it is basically clean looking most of the time, then you may want to just sweep, mop and spray buff the floor once a week instead of scrubbing it first.

This would reduce the cost to the customer, and it would also reduce the time you spend at their location doing the work. This weekly type of account could be charged anywhere from 25 to 35 cents per square foot, every week for the floor care involved.

If you are doing floor maintenance on an account that only wants service to be done, once-a-month or less often, like 4 times a year, then you would top scrub and recoat with floor finish every month or each time you are there.

Whenever you are top scrubbing a floor, you must be sure to use a mild neutral floor cleaner available at your local janitorial supply store. This type of neutral floor cleaner does not affect the floor sealer and has little effect on the floor finish when you are top scrubbing the floor.

It is simply a mild detergent for use when scrubbing. Top scrubbing the floor is simply taking off a very small amount of the old floor finish (not the sealer) and then you can put down some new floor finish. (2 to 3 coats) Basically, you are so called, dressing up the floor.

Again, you can charge anywhere from 25 to 35 cents a square foot for this type of monthly account.

Getting customers for this type of service is the best part. You don't have to spend any money on advertising. The most successful operators of this type of service business, all get their customers in the same way. They simply stop by in person to the various establishments that have V.C.T. flooring and ask to speak with the owner or the manager of the business.

Simply introduce yourself and give them a business card. Tell them that you'd like to maintain their floors for them on a regular basis. Now, wait and see what their reaction is and if they are agreeable to it, then give them a price. This is the best way to pick up new accounts for this type of service.

Just make your rounds on a regular basis and get to know the managers of establishments that have V.C.T. flooring.

A great strategy for getting new customers with this type of service business is to offer to give them a free (one time) demonstration. Offer to do a hallway or a small room for them for free as a demonstration of your work. It's worth it to get your foot in the door and get the repeat business from the account.

Make your "in person" visits and talk with the manager or the decision maker only. If necessary, when you are just starting out with this service, you can work out a deal with the customer on the price per square foot in order to get the job, as long as it is still profitable for you to be doing.

Anywhere in the price range of 25 to 35 cents per square foot is profitable to be doing. Remember that most every customer you work for will want you to come back on some kind of regular basis. You'll be building up a repeat customer base, and it adds up fast! Understand that marketing your business is an ongoing continual process. It never ends.

You can also talk with other janitorial services. Many of these companies will subcontract out the floor work on their janitorial accounts as you could also do, or they may simply put you directly in touch with office managers that need to have this service done. When you are just getting started in any kind of a service business, you will find that doing some sub-contract work for another company can still be a good source of income for you.

You should buy your own floor machine as soon as you can, but there is another way to get started. Visit several of the janitorial supply stores in your area. You can find them in the yellow pages of your local phone book.

The (buffing or scrubbing) machine is the most expensive piece of equipment that you will need to operate this business, but many of the larger janitorial supply stores will rent you a floor machine for a reasonable price. In other words, line up some work first and then rent what you need and do the job.

Preferably, you should line up 2 or more jobs or one big job, and you will still find it to be very profitable, even though you rented what you needed to do the work.

Many operators of this service started out exactly like this and accumulated equipment and supplies with each new job. Some janitorial supply stores will lease you equipment, or finance it for you with small monthly payments. Explain to them that you are going into the floor care business and just starting out.

They are an excellent source of advice and technical guidance for you, and you will find them to be very knowledgeable and helpful. After all, it is to their advantage if you are successful because you will be buying wax (floor finish) and other items from them on a regular basis.

Remember, this is a very lucrative service business. Don't let the price of a floor machine stop you when you can simply rent what you need when starting out. Many one-person floor care services, with one part-time helper, are bringing in over $100,000 dollars a year! Talk to several janitorial supply stores for more details on starting this particular service business and use this report as a guide.

You will want to get some insurance to cover any on-the-job injuries or damage that may occur. You can put off getting bonded as it is really not required of you. It's more of a selling point that you can do without.

The cost of insurance and bonding for any type of service business varies so much that you should check with several different companies and compare rates.

SOME TIPS TO REMEMBER ARE THE FOLLOWING:

Always read the instructions on the back of the containers of stripping solutions or detergent. Follow the manufacturer's instructions to the letter. Usually, it is, 1-part cleaner added to 4 parts of water or 1-part cleaning solution to 3 parts of water. Have an extra bucket available for mixing your cleaning solution in and a measuring cup always comes in handy.

When spreading out either the stripping solution or the mild detergent for scrubbing, you should do so by simply dipping the entire mop into the solution and then liberally spreading it out onto the floor. Don't ring out the mop of excess liquid, but spread it all out on the floor.

You can use a wet vac to remove the bulk of the liquid after using the floor machine. Then mop the floor 2 or 3 times with a clean mop-head and clear water to remove any residue or the floor will dry with streaks on it.

When applying the wax (floor finish) to the floor, simply place the mop-head onto the floor and then pour some floor finish onto the mop as you go, for an even looking coat of wax.

You can decide to start a service business one day and have money coming in within a week. Whatever service it is, put some effort into marketing your service business every week and stick with it! The profit potential for an owner of this type of service business (or any of the service businesses described in this kit) is very high!

You will find this training program to be very useful and practical. It will speed up your success in the office cleaning business even more.

Here is another source of information that I can recommend to you with confidence. It is "Building Service Contractors Association International." They have a paid member publication called "Services" and a free email publication called, "Smart Brief." You can sign up for "Smart Brief" on their website at http://www.bscai.org or contact them at

330 North Wabash Ave. Suite 2000
Chicago IL. 60611

The toll-free phone number is 1-800-368-3414

email: info@bscai.org

Made in the USA
Middletown, DE
02 March 2018